Clarence Tillenius on packtrain trip
with friend Andy Russell 1957

Text and compilation copyright © 1998
by Trails of the Interlake Studio
441 Dominion Street,
Winnipeg, Manitoba R3G 2M8

Artwork copyright © 1998
by Clarence Tillenius

ISBN 1-55056-618-0

cover painting - Grizzly Mother Warning Riders 24x30 oil
collection of Mr. John Crabb

Tillenius

Trail Guide

The animal shall not be measured by man. In a world older and more complete than ours they move finished and complete, gifted with extensions of the senses we have lost or never attained, living by voices we shall never hear. They are not brethren, they are not underlings, they are other nations, caught with ourselves in the net of life and time, fellow prisoners of the splendor and travail of the earth.

Henry Beston
from The Outermost House (1928) ch.2

Rocky Mountain Goats 48x24 inches oil

Autumn Mosaic - Dall Sheep 48x24 inches oil

Dall Sheep on Mountainside 20x16 inches oil

Why I Paint Wilderness

I strive through my paintings to communicate to others what has moved me deeply in nature. I believe that there is in the universe an underlying rhythm, a stream of life common to all ages; that the work of an artist who could tap into that rhythm would be timeless, it would be understood in any age, since man himself is bound by, and responds to, the same rhythm as the animals.

Art that is to endure must always derive its strength from nature; that is, the artist must have a profound understanding of, and a feeling for, the elemental sources of things, the rhythms of life that are not affected by passing fashions. In my paintings of animals and wilderness, I strive to convey what I feel about these things, to portray a wilderness world intelligible to any human being who is exhilarated by a mountain sunrise, who sees with pleasure a rabbit track across a snowy field, or who simply enjoys being outdoors. It is wrong to think that the viewer of a painting must be a connoisseur of art, or even must know how the painting was done. It is the business of the artist to perfect a technique that will communicate what he feels about what he chooses to paint.

The Manitoba Interlake country, when I was born in 1913, was then newly settled wilderness. But while I was growing up, the moose, elk, wolves, and bears were being destroyed, wiped out by the settler's ready rifle, leaving only nostalgic memories of the days when their numbers were such that no one thought they could ever disappear. So while I was young, I learned that much of the fascinating world of wildlife will always be doomed to disappear with the coming of settlement by man. I guessed that it must be so, and was determined to paint pictures that would convey what I felt about the wonderful world which I believed was slipping away.

It was with brush, pencil and pen that I was most strongly moved to try to render my fascination with wild creatures, but I also felt an urgent need to make people aware of the threats to their natural heritage. To this end , I used whatever time I could take from painting and drawing to write and lecture - always on my favourite themes: the singular beauty of animals as seen in the wild and the need to preserve their habitat.

In 1954, I began a series of large paintings of Canada's wildlife and wilderness landscapes. Many of these paintings are now grouped together in a collection in Winnipeg. Hundreds of thousands of reproductions of these paintings and their accompanying texts have been distributed across Canada and around the world. It was my hope that people who saw them would be moved to preserve some of that matchless wilderness we are now so blessed with but which will disappear unless people who care unite to safeguard it.

Discerning people have long sensed instinctively the human need for a continual renewing of mankind's bond with nature and with the earth. To me, painting wilderness is a way of saying that nature must be understood and protected by people if man is to survive in a civilized world.

In 1982, I found the right arm that I had lost so many years before and she has helped me to not only survive but to have time as I never had it before to create and many of the works on these pages would not be here without that right arm - my Penny.

Foreword

One of my earliest recollections of Clarence Tillenius was at the opening of the new Monarch Life Building in Winnipeg in 1962 when an exhibition of his work, originally held only for the benefit of Monarch Life employees, was later opened to the general public. This exhibition was well received.

Simply enjoying the beauty of Clarence's work is, in itself, a gratifying experience, but to have the added pleasure of knowing him personally and watching his work progress over the years has meant a great deal to me.

As a struggling artist in the early 1930's Clarence was thrilled to have his work recognized by "The Country Guide", which used one of his works and paid him the princely sum of $2.00. Clarence appreciated this encouragement and, as the years went by, he continued to contribute illustrations, columns, reviews and numerous paintings to be used for covers by "The Country Guide".

Because of his ardent love of nature and wildlife, Clarence has travelled extensively throughout Canada and the United States, with particular emphasis on the far north. When time and weather permitted, he sketched the animals, the changing landscape and the people of the Arctic regions and took coloured slides which he still uses in his lectures.

Learning from the work of other artists is also important to Clarence. Enjoyable and instructive visits were paid to Carl Rungius and Charlie Beil in Banff and to Allan Brooks in Vernon, British Columbia, to Harald Wiberg in Sweden and to Paul Bransom in New York. During his many trips to Europe, Clarence spent considerable time viewing and studying the works of famous artists.

As one of his many accomplishments Clarence has also enjoyed lecturing over the years at such institutions as Yale University, The Art Students' League of New York and the Society of Wildlife Art of the Nations at Sandhurst, Gloucester, England.

Probably one of Clarence's most thrilling experiences was his sponsorship by Ilia Tolstoy, grandson of the famous Russian author, Leo Tolstoy, to the Explorers Club of New York, as a Fellow. A just reward to this outstanding artist.

Among Clarence's greatest loves are his dioramas which he started in 1959. They are a tribute to his extraordinary ability to depict wild animals in their natural habitat, a skill he perfected through thousands of hours spent sketching in the wild. Clarence's dioramas can be found at the Provincial Museum in Victoria and the Canadian Museum of Nature in Ottawa and, closer to home, the dioramas in the Museum of Man and Nature which are an excellent example of his work.

Bull Moose at Sunset 20 x 28 inches oil collection of John Crabb

Country Guide Cover July 1952

Deer in Snow Flurry   12.75 x 17.75 inches   watercolor   collection of John Crabb

It is indeed significant that the newly-founded Pavilion Gallery Museum Inc. in Assiniboine Park has chosen Clarence as one of three artists to be permanently exhibited. In my view, this honour has been bestowed on him because he is respected as one of Canada's foremost nature artists.

I am confident that Clarence's extraordinary work will provide lasting enjoyment to people of all ages for generations to come and will be a great addition to the cultural heritage of our City and Province.

John Crabb.

John Crabb and Clarence Tillenius at the Winnipeg Sketch Club 1996

7

Far left Tillenius at logging camp 1934

Christopher Swenson, great-grandfather to Clarence Tillenius born Nov.19, 1830 died Jan.18 1926. At age 71 came to the Interlake country in Manitoba to homestead.

Front row far left is Clarence Tillenius in grade one at Clematis School 1919. His teacher was Marion Archibald (Irwin) - back row far right -and they have kept in correspondence through all the years.

Tillenius choosing site for grizzly diorama 1961

First pencil sketch when in hospital after losing arm

Biography

For more than thirty years Father Van de Velde at Hall Beach in the High Arctic shared the lives of the Inuit. He knew better than any other white man the awesome silences, the grim severities, the consummate thrills of these limitless horizons. In writing of the painting of the polar bear by Clarence Tillenius, the quiet priest summoned words that others might not have found.

*" We contemplate and anticipate it coming out of its frame; it is an intellectual delight. Photographs of the same subject, however beautiful, do not produce the same spiritual feeling. The picture of the white bear passes through the living intelligence and imagination of Tillenius, who while communing with his subject, reproduces it alive." *1*

In his article *Listen to the Wild*, Richard Savage wrote:

*" Tillenius is one of the finest painters of wild life our country has produced. But he is more than this. Explorer, lecturer, teacher, photographer and writer, he has risen to a rigid integrity that tolerates no compromise. He does not imagine his subjects, he lives with them, senses their innermost feelings, expathizes and then distills their essence into the deft lines and subtle shadings that characterize his art" *2*

This talented Manitoban , born in 1913, has contributed so much to our Canadian heritage through his art and works ardently to preserve our matchless wilderness. Dr. Ian MacLaren referred to Clarence Tillenius as:

*"...the dean of Canadian Wildlife painters, a Canadian treasure whose worth to us increases by the year, and stands to continue doing so long after we have left this world to our children and the buffaloes." *1a.*

subjects, which range from the grizzly of the Yukon to the caribou of Newfoundland, from the buffalo of the rolling western prairies, to the muskox on their stamping grounds in the Barren Lands, and on to the majestic polar bear whose home is the ice-floes of the Arctic, literally come alive on canvas. Tillenius' sketches, paintings and dioramas are the product of years of close association with and careful observation of animals in their natural habitat. With fluid brushwork that suggests rather than renders detail, Tillenius portrays animals in their native environment and creates the illusion of actually being at the place represented.

Despite the loss of his painting arm in a construction accident in 1936, Clarence Tillenius never relinquishes his efforts to capture on canvas the fascinating world of wildlife gradually disappearing under the pressure of civilization. Tutored by a fine artist and great friend, Alexander Musgrove, he mastered the use of his left hand - and went on to complete some of his most ambitious and successful undertakings. Some of his most diverse and widely followed work was done for the publication *The Country Guide.* Their readership in 1958 of 300,000 subscribers each month followed the young artist's career as if he was one of their own. Tillenius work was seen on many covers and his columns *Sketch Pad Out-of-Doors* and *Through Field and Wood* were popular for their content as well as the skilled drawings. Tillenius painted the first cover that *The Country Guide* reproduced in 1935 (little did he know at that time he was to lose the arm he painted it with less than a year later.) But with courage and

A keen student of nature since his childhood days in the Manitoba Interlake region, Clarence Tillenius devotes his life to painting all species of Canadian wildlife. His

top: Ivan Eyre and Clarence Tillenius lower left :Bill Mayberry, Jordan Van Sewell, Clarence Tillenius, Leo Mol

Nature in Ottawa, and Manitoba's Museum of Man and Nature in Winnipeg. The latter saw his long-nurtured interest in buffalo which used to wander in millions across the prairies, reach a climax when he completed a fifty-one foot diorama depicting a Red River Buffalo Hunt for the opening of the museum by her Majesty Queen Elizabeth. Tillenius has completed eighteen dioramas.

In 1993 a selection of seventy of his buffalo paintings was a featured exhibit at the Provincial Museum of Alberta in Edmonton. Titled *Days of the Buffalo*, it ran for the months of June and July. The enthusiastic comments of visitors from almost every country on the globe filled four large guest books.

undying patience he began painting once more and *The Country Guide* published his first cover painted with the left hand in 1940. His covers, articles and drawings were featured in this magazine until the mid 1960's when Tillenius accepted a contract to do several large dioramas for the National Museum of Natural Sciences in Ottawa (now the Canadian Museum of Nature.)

Starting in 1954, the Monarch Life Assurance Company annually commissioned paintings by Tillenius which were made into high quality reproductions. Any of their customers that wished could fill out a form and receive these prints. Over a million were distributed world wide over the years. A section on this collection appears elsewhere in this book.

Creating dioramas: (a combination of background landscape with foreground

In 1994 Tillenius produced a painting which was chosen

animal mounts) were a major part of Tillenius's career. He created dioramas for the British Columbia Provincial Museum in Victoria, the Alberta Provincial Museum in Edmonton, the Canadian Museum of

for the cover of a music CD by Andrew Roblin. The CD is titled after the Tillenius painting *Perilous Pursuit*. The artist soon will be working on a cover painting for an upcoming children's music CD composed by Mr. Roblin.

1995 saw a successful retrospective exhibit at Loch & Mayberry Fine Art Inc. gallery with over 1400 people attending the opening of the exhibit. Over one hundred and twenty-five works sold. The work on display covered a time span of over fifty years.

Clarence Tillenius in 1996 gifted a group of his works to The Whyte Museum of the Canadian Rockies. They will be on display at various times of the year and include all the media the artist used: charcoal, pen and ink, pencil, dry brush, watercolours and oil paintings.

In 1998 he began work on a diorama of the Inuit hunting caribou from their kayaks as the caribou crossed the

Clarence Tillenius and President and Chief Executive Officer of the Canadian Museum of Nature Joanne V. DiCosimo in Ottawa,1997
2. Bill Mayberry, Tillenius, Alan Sapp, John Kurtz 1997 3. Richard Calver, Ivan Eyre, Tillenius 1998

lower Kazan River 75 to 100 years ago, for the Cultural Heritage Centre in Baker Lake, N.W.T. Tillenius was on hand when it was officially opened by the Elders of Baker Lake, and Their Excellencies, the Govenor General of Canada, Mr. Romeo LeBlanc and Mrs. Diana Fowler LeBlanc, on June 3, 1998.

Founding Member of the Society of Animal Artists of New York, and of the Society for Wildlife Art of the Nations (SWAN) in England, Tillenius was also elected Fellow to the prestigious Explorers Club headquartered in New York in 1967, and was recently made a Fellow Emeritus. In addition, he was elected a Fellow to the Royal Geographical Society of London, U.K.; is Past President and Life Member of the Manitoba Naturalist's Society; and is a member Emeritus of the OWAA

Charlie 18x24 inches oil collection of Mr. and Mrs. George and Minnie Friesen

Muster Call - Timberwolves by Moonlight 18x24 inches oil 1984
from the collection of Mr. Justice R. Mykle and Ms. Lori McBeth

(Outdoor Writers Association of America.) He was awarded the Professional Wildlife Conservation Award by the Provincial Government of Manitoba. This award recognized Tillenius as "*... an individual who has made a significant and everlasting contribution to public understanding and appreciation of wildlife.*" It offically recognized him as one of Canada's premiere wildlife artists. The University of Winnipeg honoured Tillenius by bestowing on him an Honorary Doctorate of Laws degree in 1970.

*1. Eric Mitchell, *Canadian Artists Series; Clarence Tillenius, Nature Canada*, vol.1, 1972. publisher Canadian Nature Federation, Ottawa, (back cover Coyote and Cottontail by C. Tillenius)

* 2 .Richard Savage; *Listen to the Wild* . Published by the Okanagan Game Farm, Penticton, British Columbia.

For further information on the artist:

*1a. Discussion at greater length of Tillenius art is available in I.S. MacLaren, *Buffalo in Word and Image: from European Origins to the Art of Clarence Tillenius. in Buffalo*, ed. by John Foster, Dick Harrison, I.S. MacLaren (Edmonton: The University of Alberta Press 1992) pp. 79-129.

2. The video *Tokens of Myself - The Man and His Art* by Richard Savage (30 min.)

3. Taped interviews with CKY, CBC, PBS available on video.

4. *Days of the Buffalo* catalog for the 1993 Edmonton exhibition.

5. *Sketch Pad Out-Of-Doors* by Tillenius 1956.

6. Video from CBC *Tillenius on the Prairies* 45 minutes

Clarence Tillenius receives his Doctorate from the University of Winnipeg 1970

Whitetail Buck in Old Orchard 18x24 inches oil private collection

Snowy Weather - Moose Moving to Find New Ground 15x18 inches watercolor
from the collection of the Manitoba Museum of Man and Nature donated by Justice Ivan Schultz

Foxes and Lichened Rocks 24x48 inches oil private collection

Assiniboine River Trail 24x48 inches oil

Time to Leave 20x28 inches oil collection of Mr.and Mrs. George and Minnie Friesen

April 1956

Squirrels Were Here 10x20 inches oil

The Lookout Tower 24x18 inches oil
collection of Mr.and Mrs. George and Minnie Friesen

After the Ice Ages   28x72 inches oil collection of Harry and Doneta Brotchie

Tillenius with Harry and Doneta Brotchie

Jim Ballance with artist

Cloudburst and Lightning Strike   36x72 inches oil collection of Betty Ballance and Eleanor McMillan

Coming to the Waterhole   24x48 inches oil collection of Betty Ballance

Home Ranch - Tiger Taken'em on Down 48x72 inches oil collection of the Pavilion Gallery Museum Inc.

Tillenius works from life as often as possible, working in the field and then in the studio for the details of the painting. He uses life models as shown, with the model posing to get the hand position correct for the rider.

model posing for hand positioning

The New Calf 22x36 inches oil

Pronghorns and Buffalo Fleeing Prairie Fire 24x48 inches oil

Portrait Sketch Dolly Dancer 10x13 oil circa 1930's

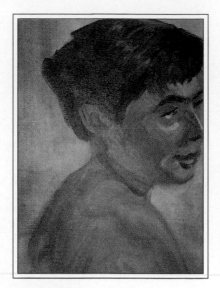

Sketch - Unknown Model 10x12 oil circa 1930's

Sketch Unknown Model 8x10" oil circa 1930's

Sketch George Paterson artist friend 10x12" oil circa 1930's

The preliminary studies on this page were all done in sittings of less than two hours and are not finished portraits.

Sketch Stu MacDonald 8x12" oil circa 1930's

Sketch Cliff Jasper 8x10" oil 1937

* all six sketches on this page are from the collection of the Pavilion Gallery Museum Inc.

Deer Coming to the Lake to Drink 24x48" oil

Rejoining the Herd 24x48" oil

Range Mothers - Grizzly and Buffalo 24x48" oil collection of the Pavilion Gallery Museum Inc.

Beaver Magazine cover 1993

The Prairies in Flower 24x60" oil private collection

Challenging Antlers 48x72" oil

On intricate designs, Tillenius often works it out in detail in charcoal on the canvas before starting to paint. The charcoal design at the left illustrates this was done for *Challenging Antlers* which the artist completed in 1998

Andrew Roblin, musician extraordinaire, and Clarence Tillenius with the painting that was used as the cover for Mr. Roblin's music CD titled **Perilous Pursuit**

Cougar Stalking Big Horn Ram 48x72" oil detail of this painting is on the back cover.

Mother Bear and Cubs Up A Tree With Packtrain in Distance
oil collection of Jotrin Investments Ltd.

Preparing for the Trail 12x18" watercolor collection of Elsie Hignell

Ascent or Descent   22x28" oil
*First painting used for a cover
from the collection of*
The Pavilion Gallery Museum Inc.

Tillenius Collection
at the
Pavilion Gallery Museum Inc.
Assiniboine Park, Winnipeg, Manitoba, Canada

This body of works is a heritage collection containing invaluable archival material. The works in the collection of the Pavilion Gallery Museum Inc. are comprehensive, significant, and representative of the many mediums and styles used by the artist: oil and watercolor paintings, black and white sketches including color notes to display the whole process, pen and ink drawings, charcoal sketches, pencil drawings and mixed media work. All, whenever possible, include the preliminary work and notes of the artist and actual issues of the publications which contain reproductions of the original art in the collection. They show the format and scope of Tillenius art and the mandate and the contribution of his art to the preservation of heritage and cultural scenes starting in the early thirties to the present date.

Tillenius's art reproduction started with the first painting, Ascent or Descent (painted in 1934) used for a *Country Guide* cover in 1935. This first cover was painted by the artist using his right hand. After he lost his right arm in a construction accident in 1936, the relationship continued with Tillenius selling the idea for a cover painting to the *Guide* in 1937 - but due to losing his arm he was not yet sufficiently adept enough with painting skills to execute the painting himself, so they bought the idea and had Lynn Bogue Hunt in New York carry out the idea. It wasn't until 1940 that Tillenius had mastered his skill well enough to once again see his original oil painting, a boy sewing a goat harness, (painted with the left hand) on the cover of this magazine. These two oil paintings are included in this collection.

Noteworthy, that there were 300,000 subscribers in 1958[1] in order to understand the wide-spread impact that Tillenius art had through The *Country Guide*. 300,000 people seeing Tillenius art and reading his thoughts and feelings every month - an overwhelming thought. These subscribers felt he paid them a visit once a month; was one of them; was *family* . The covers by Tillenius were waited for with anticipation as many people collected them and sometimes hung them on the walls. At exhibitions people have brought scrapbooks that they have saved all these years which have as many of the covers as they could keep, as well as illustrations and news stories and interviews.

By using the artwork the way this magazine did - featuring it on the covers, using it for illustration in the body - they showed initiative and imagination in bringing something to their readership that was, in many cases, without radio, power, telephone or TV. It was a vital link to the outside world. The editor, Mr. Chipman, in the early years, set out to change the magazine into a highly illustrated one.[2] This allowed the Tillenius talent to be used to its

Boy and Goat 20x26" oil
*First painting used as a cover painted with the left hand
from the collection of The Pavilion Gallery Museum Inc.*

greatest effect. Born on a homestead in 1913 in the Interlake region, Tillenius not only depicted this way of living in his art, but it was also the life that he lived. During these first years Clarence Tillenius went from submitting paintings for the covers of The *Country Guide* to being the art editor when the then editor Col. Abel was relieved of the position so he could participate in the World War II. Tillenius held this position until the late forties, when Col. Abel returned. During this time Tillenius not only submitted work for the covers but also edited and wrote and illustrated columns and illustrated many articles and stories. After the return of Col. Abel, Tillenius kept on providing paintings and writing columns and illustrating stories.

Sketch Pad Out-of-Doors was a series of columns (well over 125) which Tillenius wrote and illustrated. These columns were made into a book which has been published three times (the first two editions sold out). Original drawings and illustrations from this series are reproduced in this book.

Through Field and Wood , the next series of articles and columns (47 in all) written and illustrated by Clarence Tillenius for The *Country Guide*. Original artwork from these issues, which ranged from 1958 to 1962, are also to be found on the following pages.

The book *The First Fifty Years* published by United Grain Growers in 1957 deals with the history of the U.G.G. and its publishing of *The Country Guide*. This book has throughout its content line-cut drawings by Clarence Tillenius. From these drawings Tillenius worked up watercolours to form a collection called *The Homestead Days*. The black and white line-cut and then the colour watercolour paintings depicting farm life in the early days, showing threshing, wood hauling, and farm life in general are seen here.

Over and above the cover artwork and the two columns *Sketch Pad Out of Doors* and *Through Field and Wood* - many stories and articles contained in the body of the magazine were illustrated by Tillenius. This relationship carried on into the mid-1960's when Tillenius accepted a contract to do several large dioramas at the National Museum in Ottawa and provincial museums which kept him so busy that he was not able to continue.

Other pieces in the collection were published in magazines across the continent such as: *Nature Magazine (Washington, D.C.),The Montreal Standard, Weekend Picture Magazine, Virginia Wildlife, Star Weekly, Sports Afield (New York), Fur Trade Journal, Saturday Night, Rod and Gun, Game and Fish Magazine, Pelli and Pellicce, Esperanto Magazine*. One magazine that Tillenius contributed to for over forty years was *The Beaver*.

His book illustrations include: *Little Giant* by Olive Knox, published by Ryerson Press, Toronto, *North of "55"* by C.P. Wilson, *Kirby's Gander* by J.P. Gillese, *Furbearers of Canada* published by Hudson's Bay Co., *Brief History of the Hudson's Bay Co., What's Ahead for Prairie Agriculture* by H.S. Fry, <u>The First Fifty Years</u> by R.D. Colquette, *Sketch Pad Out-of-Doors* by C.I. Tillenius, *Tomorrow is for You* by Vera Kelsey, Scribner's New York, *Orphan of the North* by Will Henry, Random House, New York, *Black Falcon*, by

Boy with Lambs 20x26 oil
collection of The Pavilion Gallery Museum Inc.

Mare, Colt and Boy 20x26" oil
collection of The Pavilion Gallery Museum Inc.

Boy Overlooking Elk Herd 20 x26 oil

Nude Study circa 1930's
collection of the Pavilion Gallery Museum Inc.

Olive Knox, Bouregy and Curl, New York, *Encyclopedia Canadiana* (10 volumes) The Grolier Society, Ottawa, *Game Birds and Animals of Manitoba*, Government of Manitoba, *Deer Hunting Hints* by C.I. Tillenius, Canadian Industries Ltd.

In the early years of his career Tillenius and fellow artists such as Peter Kuch and Leo Mol got together once a week to do life drawings and portraits. Many of these early works are in the Pavilion permanent collection.

Other art, painted from journeys throughout the continent, is more recent and makes the span of the collection from - 1934 to 1998 - sixty-four years.

*1. R.D. Colquette ,*The First Fifty Years *,a history of the United Grain Growers page 293 and*2 page 83.

Photo by Jack Ablett
of Peter Kuch (left) and Clarence Tillenius (right)

Nude Study circa 1930's
collection of the Pavilion Gallery Museum Inc.

Wolf Field Sketches 14x18" oil
collection of the Pavilion Gallery Museum Inc.

Elephant Herd 18x25" pen and ink
collection of Mr. Jorden Morris

Deep Woods Broadcaster - Red Squirrel Scolding Blackbear 48x72" oil

Whitetailed Deer at Hawks Slough 48x72" oil collection of the Pavilion Gallery Museum Inc.

preliminary sketch for painting

Mare Colt and Dog 22x24" oil circa 1930's collection of The PAvilion Gallery Museum Inc.

The preliminary pencil sketch used to work out the design for the cover of the Country Guide August 1944 and the finished design on the cover above. Both pieces are in the collection of the Pavilion Gallery Museum Inc.

The four reproductions show the the finished work a close-up and
preliminary work and the actual tearsheet from the magazine

All the Tillenius works shown here are from
the collection of the Pavilion Gallery
Museum Inc.

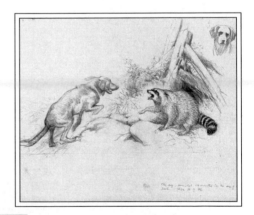

The Mists of Autumn 24x48" oil private collection

Rivals on the Marsh 27x36" oil collection of Jotrin Investments Ltd.

Dangerous Prey 16x20" oil collection of Mr. Lloyd J. Simmons

Moose on Buffalo Marshes 27x36" oil private collection

*Preliminary design sketch in charcoal on brown paper for the
Moose diorama in the British Columbia museum
collection of the Pavilion Gallery Museum Inc.*

Caribou on the Nejanilini Barrens 20x54" oil private collection

Detail from California Bighorns in the Okanagan
collection of Jotrin Investments Ltd.

California Bighorns in the Okanagan

20x49.5 "oil collection of Jotrin Investments Ltd.

Cody Life Studies 12x24" oil

Prairie Sky and Pronghorns 36x48 oil collection of Bruce and Joy Bower

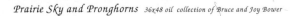

Under the Prairie Sky 18x24" oil private collection

Stone Sheep Field Sketches 16x20" oil
collection of the Pavilion Gallery Museum Inc.

Bighorn Ram Field Sketches 16x20" oil
collection of the Pavilion Gallery Museum Inc.

Mountain Goat Kids Field Sketches 16x20" oil
collection of the Pavilion Gallery Museum Inc.

Herd on a Hillside 24x36" oil from the Halter Collection

Outlook Over West Hawk 27x36" oil

Whitetails Feeding After Snow 18x24" private collection

Buck in Tamarack Swamp 18x24" oil
collection of the Museum of Man and Nature

Phragmites Hideaway 14x16" oil

Deer on Pre-Cambrian Shield 20x54" oil *collection of Marcel and Agnes Pauwelyn*

Elk Bugling in the Mountains 1959 27x36" oil

Monarchs of the Wild
and
Furbearers of Canada

**Collection of the Museum of Man and Nature gifted to them by
Manulife Financial**

At a dinner one night our host Dr. Tom McCarthy introduced me to his friend Dr. Cotter, librarian at St. Paul's College, who asked me if I would give his college boys a talk on wildlife painting and show some of my work.

During the talk I showed some of my private sketchbooks saying that these drawings would never be sold.

After this talk a man came up to me saying "My name is Cecil Grover, I am art director for Hignell Printing: do you mind telling me why you say those drawings shown tonight will never be sold - why then did you do them?" I replied: "Many years ago I began a project to paint all the large game animals and fur-bearers of Canada - these sketchbooks are my

working drawings for that project." He said: "Very interesting," then thanked me and left.

One or two years later came a surprise phone call from Cec Grover telling me he had discussed with the president and general manager of Monarch Life Insurance Company the project I had described: they were much interested and asked me to a meeting: they wanted me to paint the series I had outlined to Cec; they would publish a painting each year as a calendar and when the project was complete they would have a collection of animal paintings such as no insurance company had yet sponsored.

That was the inception of *Monarchs of the Canadian Wilds and Furbearers of Canada* collection.

Buffalo on Assiniboine Plains 25x36" oil 1954

The paintings reproduced on the following pages of this section with the black and white drawings adjacent are all from the collection of the Museum of Man and Nature.

Otter Sunning on Stranded Log 27x36" oil 1972

The company commissioned the first painting in 1954 called *Buffalo on Assiniboine Plains*. The project continued for the next thirty years and resulted in thirty-six oil paintings of the monarch, or male, of the species and thirty-six black and white drawings of the female and young. The collection of seventy-two works was published as high-quality reproductions and over one million were distributed. The opening of the new Monarch Life building in Winnipeg in 1962 featured a large exhibition of Tillenius' work and the guard counted the number of visitors: over thirteen thousand came to view it during the last week it was opened to the public. The ownership of the collection changed hands when the company was bought by North American Life, and later again by Manulife Financial Assurance Company. The latter company presented the collection to the Manitoba Museum of Man and Nature as a cultural gift to the people of Manitoba. The inaugural display of the total collection was at the Museum of Man and Nature in 1997. A major portion of the collection was included in a retrospective of the artist's work held at the same museum in 1998. Sixteen of the pieces were on display at the Pavilion Gallery Museum Inc. in Assiniboine Park for their inaugural exhibition in a space permanently dedicated to displaying the work of the artist. After these premiere showings, the paintings will be exhibited on a rotating basis at both institutions.

Badger Among Sand Dunes 27x36" oil 1975

Mountain Lions Hunting   *27x36" oil 1955*

Black Bear Foraging   *27x36" oil 1956*

Bull Moose Following the Herd   *27x36" oil 1957*

Red Fox in Early Snow 27x36" oil 1973

Arctic Foxes on Winter SeaCoast 27x36" oil 1979

Ermine and Feeding Sharptails *27x36" oil 1976*

The Dam Builders - Beavers at Work *27x36" oil 1978*

Prairie Jackrabbit Alert for Danger *27x36" oil 1977*

Bobcat on the Prowl 27x36" oil 1978

Lynx at Forest Den 27x36" oil 1979

Grizzly Monarch of the Mountains 25x36" oil 1965

Fisher Hunting in Winter Woods 27x36" oil 1979

Winter Evening Mink at Play 27x36" oil 1978

Friendly Greeting - Striped Skunk Visiting 27x36" oil 1977

Whitetail Deer in Autumn Woods 25x36" oil 1955

Mule Deer Browsing 27x36" oil 1960

Blacktail Deer in Coastal Forest 27x36" oil 1966

Bighorn Rams on the Divide *27x36 oil 1961*

Timberwolves Resting at Sunrise *27x36" oil 1969*

Pronghorned Antelope at the Waterhole *27x36" oil 1962*

Rocky Mountain Goats in Stormy Weather   27x36" oil 1964

Woodland Caribou at River Crossing 25x36" oil 1957

Barrenground Caribou on Migration 27x36" oil 1967

Dall Rams on Yukon Cliffs *27x36" oil 1964*

Muskoxen in the Arctic Barrens *27x36" oil 1970*

Wolverine Patrolling the Taiga *27x36" oil 1973*

Coyotes Hunting on Muskrat Marsh *27x36" oil 1977*

Raccoons Exploring a Crayfish Creek *27x36" oil 1975*

Marten on Woodpecker Tree 27x36" oil 1976

Muskrat Marsh in Autumn Mist 27x36" oil 1976

Red Squirrel's Kingdom 27x36" oil 1976

Bull Moose at Hanson's Creek 36x48" oil private collection

Defying the Pack 32x48" oil private collection Winnipeg

Portrait study of the artist's mother
Inga Tillenius 10x14" oil circa 1940's collection of the Pavilion Gallery Museum Inc.

Fleeing the Red Demon
9x12" watercolor circa 1990's

Wall of Fire
9x12" watercolor circa 1990's

Chronology

The following information has been edited from the personal journals of Clarence Tillenius.

1913 - Clarence Tillenius born in Sandridge, Manitoba to Carl and Inga Tillenius. Carl emigrated from Sweden in 1902 and homesteaded in the Interlake region: Inga came from Minnesota, her people coming from Norway two generations earlier.

1929 - Tillenius finishes high school at Teulon Collegiate. Traps, works on farms in central and western Manitoba. Logs, works in pulpwood camps in northern Manitoba and Ontario. Rides the rods looking for work during the years of the depression (thirties) and works for construction camps.

1934 - Sells first magazine cover to *The Country Guide*. Cuts railroad ties, works on forest fires and builds homestead cabin in Ontario.

1936 - January - Loses right arm on a construction job, under a CNR rock car, while working on steam shovel at Hudson, Ontario. Returns to Winnipeg and begins training left hand to draw.

1937 - Begins three and one half year study of art with Alexander J. Musgrove of Glasgow, in Winnipeg. Spends summers sketching on farms and in backwoods of Manitoba and Ontario. Returns to northern Ontario, paints landscape, workmen and animals. Sells first magazine cover painted with left hand.

1940 - Begins again to do magazine covers and illustrations in Canada and receives commissions from magazines in the United States. In Winnipeg works as the entire art department of The Central Press (a color printing firm) and doubles as acting editor of *The Country Guide* during the war years when Col. Abel, who was the editor, is away overseas.

1944-1945 - Visits Carl Rungius, famed painter of big game, in his Banff studio. Visits Allan Brooks, a painter of birds, in Vernon, B.C. Tillenius feels that he learns much from both artists.

Makes a two-thousand mile trip through the Rockies, interior British Columbia, and back and forth across the plains of Saskatchewan and Alberta accompanying H.S.Fry, then editor of *The Country Guide*. Takes a side trip to country around Brooks, Medicine Hat, Wild Horse, Cypress Hills, studies pronghorns and rattlesnake country. Travels with R.S. Painter, *The Duke of Warble*.

1948-1953 - Goes on wolf hunting expeditions into northern Ontario, Sioux Lookout, Winnipeg River, Kenora, Red Lake country, north along the Ontario-Manitoba border. Paints: *Closing In, In the Moonlight, The Wolf hunters, Surprised at the Kill, Wolves by Night, Timber Wolves by Moonlight, The Last Run, The Hunters Hunted*.

1954 - Begins series of large paintings for Monarch Life Assurance Company, Winnipeg Manitoba. Has two one-man exhibitions of paintings in London, Ontario. London Art Gallery requests an exhibition of Tillenius book and magazine illustrations. Becomes acquainted with Eleanor Roosevelt whom he considers a very gracious lady. Meets Wm.Rush, Mayor of London, former Chief of Police.

1957 - Travels by packtrain through the Rockies with Andy Russell.

1958 - Paints bighorn sheep, grizzlies in the Waterton Mountains. Reviews entire Glenbow Foundation collection of Carl Rungius paintings, sketches, drawings and photo studies: prepares comprehensive report at personal request of donor Mr. Eric Harvie.

1959 - May/June - Embarks on an expedition to Kluane district, Yukon Territory, accompanied by Andy Russell and Dick Russell. Tillenius is guided into Dall sheep country by Dr. W.A. Fuller, with the Canadian Wildlife Service, and Joe Langevin, Fire Warden and Warden of Kluane. Paints grizzlies, Dall sheep, moose, marmots, wolves, huskies, black bears and Golden Eagles. Travels through Prince George and around the Big Bend of Columbia via Revelstoke. Paints moose at Field, B.C.

November - Goes on an expedition to Lake Athabaska and Black Lake. Fond du Lac River country to choose site and paint studies for barrenground Caribou diorama for Canadian Museum of Nature, Ottawa. Stays with fur trader Gunnar Morberg, and wife Florence. Paints trappers, Indians, caribou, sled dogs, grayling. Makes several large paintings from this trip: *Barrenground Caribou on Migration* (for the Monarch Life Collection). *Dog Team on Trail.* Meets Allan Stinson who was the model for Karl in Eric Munsterhjelm's autobiographical novel *The Wind and the Caribou* which Tillenius used as his guide to the Black Lake country.

Flies several trips with Saskatchewan Wolf Patrol along the Barrens to locate wintering ground of the caribou and observe first hand methods of wolf control and probable effects.

Quizzes friend Chick Terry about his year-long trek, following caribou northward to calving grounds and back, that was commissioned by the Saskatchewan government.

1960 - Goes to New Brunswick and chooses site and paints background for Moose diorama Canadian Museum of Nature, Ottawa. Paints in Fundy Park, Herring Cove, Pointe Wolfe River, Owl Head, Joel Head, Bay of Fundy. Does several moose and new snow paintings here as well as a number of porcupine studies. Paints portrait of the park warden Jim McLaughlin.

Confers with staff at American Museum of National History in New York about dioramas.. Visits with his friend Louis Paul Jonas, expert taxidermist, at his Hudson, New York studios to talk over taxidermy for the Ottawa dioramas. Takes trips to the Huntington Galleries and the Hispanic Society to study Sorolla murals. Makes several visits to Washington, D.C. to study Mellon Collection, National gallery, Whistlers in Freer Gallery.

September - Travels to Whitehorse, then to Kluane district Yukon Territory with Stu MacDonald; chooses site, collects rams and paints background studies for Dall Sheep diorama in National Museum of Natural Sciences in Ottawa. Makes studies of wolverines, grizzlies, placer mining in Sheep Creek. *Dall Rams on Yukon Cliffs, Rams on Sheep Mountain, The Sentinel, Above Kluane, Dall Lambs,* all date from this trip. Studies Stone sheep on side trip to Muncho Lake, B.C. Stays with Jim and Betty Grant who own Highland Glen Cabins.

October - Goes to south west Saskatchewan, south eastern Alberta; finds site for Pronghorn diorama for Canadian Museum of Nature. CBC sends photographer Paul Guyot who camps with Tillenius for three weeks in the desert while filming *Tillenius on the Prairies.* Paints and studies pronghorn antelope, coyotes, jackrabbits, mule deer, rattlers. Paintings: *Pronghorn Antelopes at the Waterhole* (Monarch Life Collection) *Pronghorns Crossing Dry Coulee, Pronghorns Alert to Danger, Mule Deer Buck in Autumn Hills, Under the Prairie Sky, Indian Summer,* all date from this time.

1961 - Makes a packtrain trip with Andy Russell along the Continental Divide where British Columbia, Alberta and

Enough for Today watercolor 9x12" collection of the Pavilion Gallery Museum Inc.

Special Service 9x12" watercolor collection of the PavilionGallery Museum Inc.

Break for Lunch 9x12" watercolor collection of the Pavilion Gallery Museum Inc.

Topping Up the Load 9x12" watercolor collection of the Pavilion Gallery Museum Inc.

Books illustrated by Tillenius

1950 Illustration for Country Guide
collection of the Pavilion Gallery Museum Inc.

Whitetails Crossing Hay Road 30x24" oil

Montana meet. Paints and studies grizzlies, elk, mule deer, marmots, eagles, packhorses, cowboys. Does background painting for Grizzly Diorama, National Museum of Natural Sciences. Does several other large canvases from this trip - *Grizzly Mother, The Disputed Trail, Mountain Man, Cliff Riders.*

Through the Rockies to Vancouver, Tillenius goes to Bella Coola, B.C. where Andy and Dick Russell join him. Travels with 4 boats, 2 guides on a 50 foot Gillnetter by the Inside Pacific Passage from Bella Coola to Rivers Inlet to Owikeno Lake, Walkwash and Markell Rivers, also Neechanz, Shumahalt and Indian Rivers. Studies and photographs grizzlies on salmon streams. Paints grizzlies, coast blacktails, salmon, Bald Eagles, seals, sea lions, pilot whales. Makes a trip travelling with Cliff Kopas of Bella Coola through Rainbow Mountains (Ulgatcho Indian Country) the Kleena Kleen, Chilcotin Plains to Williams Lake, B.C.

1962 - Has a comprehensive solo exhibition in January with over 200 pieces, to celebrate the opening of the new Monarch Life Building.
July - Travels to Europe: England, France, Holland, Germany, Denmark, Sweden., Norway. In Holland attends Franz Hals centenary in Haarlem, goes back to Sweden to visit the Baltic and Dalarna in the north. Studies and makes visits to Anders Zorn home and museum and the Carl Larsson museum. Makes extended trips to study masterpieces of Bruno Liljefors of Uppsala, Sweden, an animal painter, and to visit Harald Wiberg, a famous animal painter and illustrator of Smaland, Sweden.

Studies Rembrandt and Franz Hals in Holland, Adolf Von Menzel in Germany, Rodin sculptures, drawings in France as well as Impressionist collections. Visits Scotland to see Raeburn portraits in Edinburgh, National Portrait Collection, Glasgow. Studies paintings by J.S. Sargent at the Tate Gallery, London.

1963 - Takes expedition with J.R. Shore in twin-engine Super-Widgeon to Yukon Territory for six weeks of hunting and painting. Is in Fort Nelson, Whitehorse, Kluane district and Dawson City. Paints grizzlies, sheep, moose, black bear, varying hares, owls and ptarmigan. Joe Jacquot and Russell Dickson are the guides. Paintings: *Grizzly - Monarch of the Mountains, View Over Kluane, Varying Hare - Autumn,* date from this time. Paints on Burwash Creek, Duke River, Destruction Bay, Burwash Landing and Vulcan Creek.

1964 - February - With Ralph Hedlin travels with Inuit polar bear hunters Tommy Nakoolak, Mark Nakoolak, Raymond Ningeootcheak on Southampton Island. Paints polar bear, seal, pack ice, Inuit dogs, and sledges. Polar Bear Hunting Along the Floe-Edge dates from this trip. Hunts at floe-edge beyond Native Point, Bear Island, then crosses over to Foxe Channel, towards Baffin Island, through white fox trapping areas. Sees foxes, Arctic hares, square flipper seals. Tillenius is badly frost-bitten on both trips.

June - Travels to Ottawa to work on dioramas.

July - Makes trip through South Dakota, Wyoming (is given solo exhibition in Cody, Wyoming) to Idaho. Travels with son Homer to interior of B.C. Visits with Andy Russell at Waterton Lakes, then to Stu MacDonald's ornithological camp near Clinton, B.C. Spends summer travelling and tracking cougars with Jim Dewar (dean of Vancouver Island cougar hunters) and his pack of cougar hounds. Chooses site and paints background (Little Qualicum Falls, Vancouver Island) for Cougar diorama in Canadian Museum of Nature, Ottawa. Goes back to Ottawa to work on diorama.

1964 - On Vancouver Island tracking cougars and blacktail deer with Jim Dewar. Makes studies for *Blacktail Deer in Coastal Forest* (Monarch Life Collection). Studies deer, cougars, martens and cougar hounds.

July - Travels to Vancouver from Winnipeg with Charles Guiguet and John Hermann-Blome, drives to Williams Lake to collect three California bighorn rams for the British Columbia museum. Paints studies of Fraser River, Chilcotin River, rams, badgers. Back in Vancouver with four rams and many sketches. Spends time at sea studying coast islands with helper Jack Waters. Makes a trip to Waterton Mountains and to ranches around Pincher Creek, Alberta. Begins work in Winnipeg on Buffalo Hunt diorama for Manitoba Museum of Man and Nature.

December - Takes trip to Fort St. John, Prophet and Sikanni Chief River country to find site and paint background for moose diorama for B.C. Provincial museum, collects bull moose for diorama, does much painting.

1965 - Surveys moose population along Peace River by helicopter. Gordon Gosling, chief game warden, guides Tillenius in Pink Mountain country. Goes by truck with C. Guiguet from Dawson Creek to Prince George, from there to Vancouver Island to work on dioramas. Leaves Vancouver for Calgary and visits with friend Roland Gissing, the western painter. Works up paintings when back in Winnipeg home studio.

1966 - Makes extended canoe expedition down Whitemouth River, Manitoba in spring flood time. Draws beaver, moose, old logging operations, geese, mergansers. Stays with old trapper in cabin on river.

July - Studies bison and elk in Riding Mt. National Park. Has exhibition at Fine Art Salon during Calgary Stampede.

August - Takes trips to Milwaukee and Chicago Museums. Casts rocks and paints landscape studies for diorama when in the Whiteshell Forest, Manitoba.

October - Goes to Vancouver Island for diorama work. Takes trip to Nanaimo River. Collects cow elk for museum group. Paints at Campbell River, Buttles Lake, Cathedral Grove, B.C.

December - Travels through north Mexico, Texas, Arizona, Colorado. Sketches in the desert. To Phoenix Art Centre to see C. Russell, F. Remington exhibitions. Studies mules and gorges on trip to the Grand Canyon, Colorado. Spends Christmas with Mrs. Ernest Thompson Seton at Seton Castle near Santa Fe.

1967 - Makes an extended visit to New York and visits Col. Tolstoy at the Explorers Club. Exchanges thoughts with Paul Bransom, dean of North American animal draftsmen. Elected a Fellow to Explorers Club, headquartered in New York, sponsored by his friend Col. Ilia Tolstoy, grandson of world-famed author Leo Tolstoy.

June - Studies bison while on expedition to Elk Island Park with Dick Sutton. Travels to Wood Buffalo Park, Salt River, Peace River, Sweet Grass Marshes. Does much work towards the Red River Buffalo Hunt diorama. Spends several days getting reminiscences of old buffalo herders of Wainwright Buffalo Reserve while at a Stampede in Wainwright, Alberta.

August - Spends ten days in Elk Island Park. Sketches, and takes photos of moose, elk, bison, coyotes, beaver, muskrats, fall colors and new snow. *Rain on the Marshes, Moose in Yellow Aspens,* date from this trip.
November - Works on Victoria dioramas.
December - Paints in Manitoba

1968 - In Victoria, works on dioramas. In Wood Buffalo National Park studies animals and the wolf predation on bison. Sketches and hears wardens account of the tragedy of a bison drowned falling through the ice; foxes feeding on carcass.

Springtime Calves Playing
Country Guide Cover 1952
collection of the Pavilion Gallery Museum Inc.

Calf and Frog Country Guide Cover 1948
collection of the Pavilion Gallery Museum Inc.

Bear Cubs and Wasp's Nest - Country Guide Cover circa 1940's
collection of the Pavilion Gallery Museum Inc.

photo by Jack Ablett

photo by Jack Ablett

Artist with his cat Gus
photo by Richard Harrington

April - Makes expedition with Eric Mitchell, Ralph Hedlin to Southampton Island to go with four Inuit bear hunters on polar bear hunt Has complete Arctic clothing sewn from thirty caribou skins by Akomalik of Baker Lake. Hunters Tommy Nakoolak, Sandy Sateeana, Arsene Panyuk and Toni Eecherk had four teams with forty dogs. Inuit killed three bears on this trip. Makes studies which result in polar bear diorama in the Canadian Museum of Nature.

May - In Victoria, works on dioramas.

July - With Eric Mitchell goes to Coppermine, Holman Island, Pelly Bay and various central Arctic settlements. Sees polar bears, narwal, walrus, belugas, right whales, gerfalcons. Studies muskoxen along the Thelon River, Bathurst Inlet, Bay Chimo. Makes studies for painting *Muskoxen on the Barrens* (Monarch Collection.) Tillenius and party are forced down in fog and spend three days in a tent on the tundra at Murchison River in snow and fog. There are no casualties. Sees Sandhill Cranes, Snow Geese and one white wolf.

1969 - Works on Victoria dioramas, moose group, ram group, Roosevelt elk and Coastal Forest group.

March - On Alberta plains sees pronghorn antelope herds. Works on Buffalo Hunt diorama and Pronghorn diorama when back in Winnipeg. Chooses site for Manitoba Pronghorn diorama - the Souris River and Turtle Mts.

July - In Victoria, works on dioramas.

August - Travels through Arctic with Eric Mitchell. Goes to Churchill, Chesterfield Inlet, Repulse Bay, Igloolik, Hall Beach, Admiralty Inlet, Moffat Inlet, Arctic Bay, Pangnirtung, Frobisher Bay, interior of Baffin Island, Lake Harbour, Cape Dorset, Coral Harbour, Eskimo Point, Lynn Lake, and The Pas. Sees practically all Arctic animals on this long trip. Renews acquaintances with many of his Inuit friends. Buys narwhal tusk from Kudluk who was chief of Inuit band when they executed Soosee, an Inuit magic woman who was mad.

October to December - After a trip to Ontario and Quebec works on Manitoba dioramas.

1970 - Finishes Pronghorn diorama and Buffalo Hunt diorama in time for the opening of the Manitoba Museum of Man and Nature by her Majesty Queen Elizabeth 11, July - Honorary doctorate, University of Winnipeg. Short trip with world-famous photographer Ernst Haas to Elk Island to work among bison.

August - Expedition through the Arctic with Eric Mitchell; to Pangnirtung, Broughton Island, Clyde River, Pond Inlet. Begins preliminary work for two more dioramas in the Canadian Museum of Nature.

1971 - Travels to New Orleans, Galveston, Houston, Dallas, Ft. Worth, Tulsa, Oklahoma City (on the way stops at museums to see Remington and Russell paintings.) Leaves for Ottawa: begins Polar Bear diorama and Wood Bison diorama. Takes expedition to Wood Buffalo National Park to make additional studies and collects foreground material for Wood Buffalo diorama. Travels up and down Peace River by boat, among herds of swimming buffalo. Goes by bombardier across the Sweet Grass Marshes. He has many adventures on this trip.

1972 - Finishes Ottawa dioramas, returns to Winnipeg. Travels to Frobisher Bay, Resolute, then by single engine Otter on skis to Bathurst Island. Studies muskox herds, Arctic wolves, foxes. Only companion in camp is Dave Gill, and radio communication is poor. A white wolf *Bloodface* and *Elmer* the fox come to his camp.

July - In Banff and Jasper looks at sites for Rocky Mt. Goat diorama for Alberta Provincial Museum in Edmonton.

August - Goes to Wolverine River, Nejanilini Lake, North West Territories, and Manitoba to choose site and paints background studies for Barrenground Caribou diorama in Manitoba Museum of Man and Nature. Makes many sketches and paintings here but finds the blackflies a terror to man and beast. Travels by canoe and on foot. Tillenius finds hundreds of old caribou roads as this had been a caribou migration route for uncounted generations.

September - Travels again to Jasper and Banff. Paints background studies for goat diorama for Alberta Provincial Museum. He has adventures with sheep, coyote, elk and black bear. A snow storm traps Tillenius in the mountains. He makes many oil studies and sketches on this trip. A seven hundred pound grizzly smashes a cabin at Johnson's Canyon and a black bear kills a doe.

November - Returns to Winnipeg to work on Monarch Life paintings. Goes to Milwaukee and Chicago to confer with taxidermist on mounting of six caribou for Manitoba diorama. Studies dioramas in Field Museum, Chicago.

December - Sketches snake fences in Lanark County, near Ottawa. Paints many paintings. Attends a conference with officials from the Canadian Museum of Nature in Ottawa then returns to Winnipeg for Christmas.

1973 - Works on canvases: *Red Fox in Early Snow, Wolverine on the Taiga,* for Monarch Collection. Finishes *Bull Moose at Creek Crossing* (collection of Dr. T.G. McCarthy, Wpg.) and sends it to New York for Society of Animal Artists Exhibition.

February - Attends Trappers Festival at The Pas, Manitoba. Asked to present the bronze plaque that he designed in 1960 to the winner of the North American Dog Race. While there Tillenius shares a room with Howie Larke of Labatt's and Don Jonas of the Blue Bombers.

March - E.H. Mitchell writes a feature article for *Nature Magazine* on Tillenius.

Snowshoes on trip to Riding Mt. National Park with Joe Robertson. Flies to Edmonton to recommence work on Goat diorama in Provincial Museum.

Attends conference at Manitoba Museum of Man and Nature regarding the Barrenground Caribou diorama. Drives to Fargo, North Dakota to receive citation from the Red River Valley Historical Assoc. Leaves for Churchill on Arctic expedition with Eric Mitchell. Visits old friend Father Didier, and Inuit at Repulse Bay. At Hall Beach, visits Akatsiak who killed polar bear for the Manitoba Museum of Man and Nature diorama. Goes to Arctic Bay and Grise Fiord. Abraham Piajimeennie takes Tillenius to meet four Greenland hunters who are there on a visit. Makes expedition to Thule (Kanak) Greenland (under the Danish government) where Tillenius is shown around by a Danish-English speaking Greenlander. Here Tillenius notes that the life style is quite different from that of the Canadian Inuit.

Flies from Kanak over Bylot Island to Pond Inlet then to Clyde River where he hires a dog team. Arrives in Pangnirtung where he meets Dorothy Todd and cameraman Barry Simpson who are there making films for Sesame Street. Gets to Frobisher Bay after being held here for eight days by storms and fog, on April 29. Tide goes out and stone in sand punctures pontoon. More delay preventing landings for re-fuelling. Loads three drums fuel on plane, pilot and co-pilot rig gas line and pump out through window to refuel in midair. Plane takes off. Pilot goes

Tillenius enjoys lecturing to school children about the days of the buffalo and his trips to the north and finds their questions remarkable.

His mobile studio, a three quarter ton truck with camper, is home away from home complete with shade unbrella for painting wherever he stops.

Working in the field

Tillenius with his long time friend, Kraka Lundegard (daughter of Bruno Liljefors) at her home in Sweden.

Dr. Allan Ellenius, Dr. Hans Henrik Brummer and Dr. C. Tillenius in front of a portrait of Bruno Liljefors painted by Anders Zorn at the opening of the Liljefors exhibition in Stockholm, Sweden in 1996.

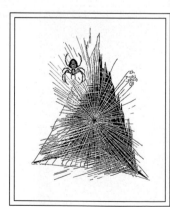

Spider Web 5.38x6.75" pen and ink 1942
collection of Robert and Margaret Hucal

Phoebe Returning 8x10.38" pen and ink
collection of Robert and Margaret Hucal

Whippoorwill 4.63x8.5" carbon pencil on paper 1941
collection of Robert and Margaret Hucal

higher to clear off icing. As plane gains altitude fuel drums begin to spout fountains of fuel as the drums are too full and the fuel expands at seven thousand feet. They have a rugged time stopping the leaks and it is one of the *hairiest* situations Tillenius encounters. Doug Lamb is the pilot. Flies clear across Hudson Bay which is in dense fog, lands at Rankin Inlet, refuels and goes on to Churchill to refuel at midnight. Is held up by a neurotic hangar mechanic before they fly on to Thompson.

Finishes *Red Fox in Early Snow, Wolverines Patrolling the Taiga,* and delivers them to Monarch Life.

Writes comprehensive article on Carl Rungius for *Leisure* magazine. Is guest speaker for Women's Institute at their annual convention at the University of Manitoba. Lectures on wildlife painting and wilderness expeditions.

Travels in camper to Edmonton to work on dioramas. Flies to Ottawa for conference, then goes to Montebello, Quebec for a reunion at Sedbergh School where his painting *Edge of the Barrens* is presented to Vera and Thomas Wood on their fiftieth wedding anniversary.

Back in Edmonton, works on diorama.

Travels to Penticton, B.C. where he sets up wildlife drawing classes at the Okanagan Game Farm for the Okanagan Summer School of the Arts.
Collects material for Rocky Mountain Goat diorama on the way to Penticton. Began teaching some forty students that eventually joined the class. Two of them are the Inuit couple that the N.W.T. government sent at Tillenius' request. Many episodes with tigers, bears, and rattlesnakes occur.

August - Leaves Penticton, drives to Banff, does sketching at Mt. Bourgeau. Then goes on to Calgary to study Bob Scriver's *Rodeo* sculptures. Drives to Edmonton and flies to Wolfville, N.S. for Canadian Nature Federation Convention. Takes trips around Nova Scotia. Visits Halifax Museum has conference with taxidermist Lloyd Duncanson. Goes to Peggy's Cove. Drives through New Brunswick, Quebec, Montreal to Ottawa. Flies to Edmonton to work on diorama.

Confers with Walter Pelzer of Milwaukee, Wisc. on mount of polar bear for his diorama in the Manitoba Museum of Man and Nature.Painting portrait of Linda Taylor (wife of helper Tom Taylor.) Nature Canada asks for (and receives) permission to use Tillenius' owl and young porcupine drawings for their promotional literature.

October - Lectures in Edmonton to Bird Club on Arctic travels. Leaves Edmonton, flies to Winnipeg to arrange for Arctic trip. Confers with Manitoba Museum of Man and Nature regarding floor plan for polar bear diorama. Flies to Churchill, stays with Mary and Joe Campayre. Joe borrows fire marshal's skidoo and sled and they leave for Knight's Hill on seacoast. R.C.M.P. say to take rifles because of the dangerous polar bears. Sleeps in gunnery observation tower on frozen fox guts: nearly freezes to death on this trip. Sketches, photographs and wanders over seacoast. Is visited by Voisey boys on skidoo who have seen she-bear with two cubs, red fox, black fox and crossfox. Joe tells story about Tootoo and the rocket recovery. (If you are curious to hear the story, ask Tillenius the next time you see him in the Pavilion Gallery Museum Inc.)

Arrives in Winnipeg with all Arctic material, sketches, photos, and polar bear notes. *Bull Moose at Creek Crossing* arrives back from Animal Artists New York Show.

Works on diorama in Edmonton.

December - gives slide show and lecture on Arctic travel and

Shift in the Wind - Deer in the Canyon 24x48" oil private collection

Buffalo Wolves Sighting the Herd 36x48" oil collection of Rock Creek Holdings

Moose and Wolves by Moonlight 36x 48" oil private collection

Susan Stobart and Wayne Rogers with Clarence Tillenius

Into The Sunset - Last of the Great Herds 36x48" oil collection of Susan Stobart and Wayne Rogers

Battle of Champions 24x48" oil collection of Mr.and Mrs. George and Minnie Friesen

Siesta By The Beach 27x36" oil

painting at University of Manitoba. Sketches deer and coyotes in the Interlake. Has conference with Harold Thompson, president of Monarch Life, on painting project and setting up joint museum retrospective exhibition

1974 - 1984
Finishes the Rocky Mountain Goat diorama in the Alberta Museum early 1974. Travels widely, viewing art collections all over the United States. Visits with Bob Scriver in Montana. Directs the animal drawing courses for the Okanagan Summer School of the Arts from 1973 to 1982. Begins a series of hand produced lithographs on stone: twelve in the series.

Makes expeditions to: the Florida Everglades, California, Montana, North and South Dakota, Kansas. Travels with several students to Sweden to study the works of Bruno Liljefors, Anders Zorn, Carl Larsson. Visits his friend the famous animal painter and illustrator Harald Wiberg, and his wife Christina. Travels to Rome, Venice, Pisa, Florence, San Michele, and the Bay of Naples to study the masterpieces of the Renaissance.

Completes the dioramas of Polar Bear, Barrenground Caribou, and the massive Boreal Forest Moose for the Manitoba Museum of Man and Nature. Holds two highly successful one-man exhibitions in 1980 and 1983. Completes the final works for Monarch Life's seventy-two piece collection of his paintings.

Lectures to the Art Students League in New York, to audiences at Yale University, and to museum groups in several provinces. Becomes a trustee of The Manitoba Wildlife Foundation. Completes a film documentary on his life in 1978 (re-edited in 1984) and several television interviews.

1984-1998

In 1984 goes on a painting expedition along the Monterey Coast painting the sea, whales, sea lions, elephant seals, and sea otters. Monarch Life Collection is displayed at Polo Park for Wildlife Week. Has exhibition at MGM Grand in Las Vegas with Wildlife Safari International. In September attends a seminar of animal artists in Jackson Hole , Wyoming. Has a large one-man 1983 exhibition in Calgary; Andy Russell gives opening talk. December studies wolf packs in the Riding Mountains.

Has successful solo exhibition in Winnipeg in 1984 of oils and watercolors. Overwhelming response to an 1985 exhibition of works on paper many of the illustrations done over the years; over 200 displayed. Harald Wiberg, Swedish artist, becomes the ower of the invitation piece which was a watercolor of a calf. Holds smaller exhibitions, at his studio, over the next few years, while he works on his buffalo collection.

Is made a *Fellow* of the Royal Geographical Society, London, England. Sponsored by the President of the Explorers Club Dr. John Levinson. Makes a trip to London to visit the Soclety Headquarters and visits the art galleries and museums in London. Travels throughout the country to visit and study Alfred Munnings' paintings.

Back in Canada travels to the buffalo parks; studies buffalo. Spends weeks in Elk Island National Park where the wardens allow him unrestricted access to the herds of Wood and Plains bison there. This culminates in a large exhibition being given by the Alberta Provincial Museum titled "Days of the Buffalo" which runs for several months and attracts thousands of visitors in 1993. The catalog for this show *Days of the Buffalo* is published. Tillenius donates a large buffalo hunt painting to the Museum of Alberta. The Museum of Man and Nature asks Tillenius for a retrospective exhibit for 1998. Work is started on this project.

Visits Dr. John and Carlie Levinson at their *Puddleby-on-the-Marsh* haven in Delaware; sketches and paints while there.

Taken by Richard Harrington on trip in the wild rice fields in the 1950's.

exhibition of illustrations

early exhibition

California coast is a favorite destination for some painting around Carmel.

At his home on the Assiniboine River with his cat Baz-Man, who sits by his easel for hours watching the paint go on.

Flies to England for the opening of the Society of Wildlife Art of the Nations (S.W.A.N.) of which he is a Founding Member. The collection is kept at Wallsworth Hall in Glouchester.

Loch and Mayberry Fine Art Inc. holds an extensive retrospective in Winnipeg in December of 1995 which receives unprecedented reviews and response. Mr. Ted Hart of the Whyte Museum of the Rockies flies from Banff, Alberta to view this exhibit (he had also been in Edmonton for the buffalo exhibit). Tillenius meets with Mr. Hart in Banff and a comprehensive collection of Tillenius works is put together of close to 100 pieces and is gifted to the Whyte Museum in 1996.

Tillenius completes a book of his travels and experiences over the years; illustrated in black and white. Hopes to have this published before the turn of the century. He works on autobiography.

Makes several trips a year to New York to study art collections and the dioramas in African Hall at the Museum of Natural History. While in New York he lectures at the Explorers Club and attends their meetings and lectures; gives slide show and lecture at The Art Students League at the invitation of his friend artist Tom Fogarty His library grows during these years to almost seven thousand books.

Tillenius visits Sweden two or three times a year to study and paint; he finds the country similar to Canada in several areas. Visits with Bruno Liljefors' daughter Kraka on each visit. Over the next few years Attends the Bruno Liljefors exhibit (travelling) which opens in New York and then follows it to the Bell Museum in Minneapolis. Hosts visit to Zoo for Herr Dr. Allan Ellenius, a professor at the University of Uppsala, who is visiting from Sweden and then to the final exhibition in Gothenberg, Sweden where Tillenius is an honoured guest and speaker at the opening ceremonies. Attends the large exhibition for Liljefors at Stockholm, Sweden 1996 (makes two trips to Sweden in 1996).

1997 Assiniboine Park Pavilion project is planned. Pavilion to open 1998.

Attends 85th. birthday celebration of Canadian Museum of Nature in Ottawa - lectures public and staff on dioramas.

1998 asked by Inuit Cultural Heritage Centre in Baker Lake, N.W.T. to create diorama of Inuit hunting caribou from kayaks on the lower Kazan River. Background painting is four feet by fifteen feet. Completes this eighteenth diorama of his career, and attends opening in Baker Lake on June third by their excellencies, the Governor General of Canada, Mr. Romeo LeBlanc and Mrs. Diane Fowler LeBlanc.

Swedish Press Interviewing Tillenius in Gothenberg, Sweden in 1989

Tillenius with buffalo "Cody" used in the movie "Dances with Wolves"

Cougar and Kittens 48x72" oil

Often the design and layout of the painting is done on a small preliminary sketch in oil on canvas which is then used as a guide for the larger composition as shown here.

preliminary sketch for the larger painting

Caribou On the Move 36x72" oil

The above four photos show the Boreal Forest diorama in Winnipeg in different stages of completion. The one immediately above shows the way the preliminary sketches were set up and used in doing the actual diorama.

Dioramas

by

Clarence Tillenius

Dioramas, for those not familiar with their construction, are large hollow shells (like a hollow ball cut in quarters) on which are painted realistic landscape backgrounds. In front of these curved backgrounds are placed the mounted animals in their home terrain of bushes, trees, rocks, prairies, ice-floes, or other landscape materials: the whole effect causing the spectator to imagine that he or she is looking at animals in their natural setting. One test of the artist's skill is that the spectator should not be able to divine where the real foreground merges with the painted background. My own experiences, augmented by the years of exchanging ideas with the many master diorama artists who became my friends, gradually enabled me to meet and solve the many and often unforeseen challenges of doing these complicated museum dioramas. The creating of these dioramas, and the wilderness expeditions they made necessary, have been a great source of pleasure over the years.

Of the eighteen dioramas I have created over my lifetime, probably the most demanding (if one excepts Manitoba's big Boreal Forest Moose diorama) was the large Red River Buffalo Hunt diorama, which at the request of the directors of the Manitoba Museum of Man and nature, I completed in time for the Museum's opening on July 15, 1970 by her Majesty Queen Elizabeth 11.

For this Buffalo Hunt diorama with which I was preoccupied for over five years from first conception to eventual completion, I made trips to most of the major buffalo ranges (where sometimes the buffalo wardens staged stampedes of several hundred buffalo so that I could experience standing in the path of a stampeding buffalo herd.) I made numerous sketches, took movies and photographs, collected sod, prairie grasses and shrubs, made casts of rocks from the untouched prairie buffalo range: and finally, aided by master taxidermist Walter Pelzer and hard-working artist Jim Carson and with the cooperation of the museum staff, the exhibit was completed as the major show piece for the museum's opening.

My involvement with dioramas, however, began much earlier. During the 1930's and 40's I had travelled to the United States visiting major natural history museums, studying such diorama collections as the great African and North American Halls in the American Museum of Natural History in New York and along the way becoming acquainted with some of the famed diorama artists: Francis Lee Jacques, Carl Rungius, James Perry Wilson, William Treher, Belmore Browne and a host of others.

So when at a convention of the Learned Societies in Winnipeg (about 1958 or '59) I was asked by Frank Banfield of the National Museum in Ottawa, if I would be interested in undertaking several dioramas - moose, Dall sheep, pronghorn antelope, and Barrenground caribou, I accepted without hesitation. I must confess, though, in retrospect, that I did have a few misgivings about how I, having lost my right arm, would manage the climbing up and down and painting from the platforms of the teetering twelve foot scaffolding required for doing the skies in these sixteen to twenty foot high diorama shells.

However, as with most projects tackled with vigour and enthusiasm, ways were found to cope with all of these obstacles, and gradually, the list of museums displaying my dioramas grew: The National Museum of Natural Sciences now the Canadian Museum of Nature in Ottawa, where Mammal Hall had eight - the Moose, Dall Sheep, Barrenground Caribou, Grizzly, Polar Bear, Pronghorn Antelope, Cougar and Wood Bison groups: the British Columbia Provincial Museum in Victoria where I produced the Moose, California Bighorn and Coastal Forest Roosevelt Elk dioramas; the Alberta Provincial Museum in Edmonton had my Rocky Mountain Goat diorama; and the Manitoba Museum of Man and nature in Winnipeg which houses five of my dioramas; the Barrenground Caribou, the Red River Buffalo Hunt, the Pronghorn Antelope, the Polar Bear and the Boreal Forest Moose diorama; the Baker Cultural and Heritage Centre in Baker Lake, North West Territories, has my most recent diorama - Inuit Hunting Caribou on the Lower Kazan River which I completed in the spring of 1998.

The above two photos are of the Polar Bear Diorama in Ottawa.

For the Vancouver Island cougar diorama I spent several months with famed cougar hunter Jim Dewar, and his pack of cougar hounds, trailing cougars by day and by night, studying their habits and finding their kills, painting the landscape backgrounds, listening fascinated to Jim's stories of a lifetime spent among the cougars.

For both the Polar Bear dioramas - in Ottawa and in Winnipeg - I made many expeditions into the Arctic to collect the knowledge I needed. Sometimes with friends Ralph Hedlin and Eric Mitchell, sometimes with Joe Campayre, with Barney Lamm, with Francis Einarson, with Doug Lamb. I flew throughout the North, watched polar bears, belugas, narwhals, walrus, seals, caribou, wolves, and Arctic foxes, had many "close calls" flying into Arctic snowstorms, overshooting primitive air strips in blizzards, or

The Moose diorama in Ottawa is shown in the above two photos.

wings icing up, when a fall into the pack-ice below meant instant death... vastly exciting dramas, all to be endured to bring those paintings and dioramas into existence.

The master taxidermists who prepared the mounted animals for the mammal groups - Louis Paul Jonas of Hudson, New York, Walter Pelzer of Milwaukee, Wisc., John Herman-Blome of Vancouver, B.C. all became close friends and together we worked out the animal groupings for the various museums.

The wilderness expeditions to locate a dramatic and paintable diorama site, and to make the sketches and to collect the material needed, have given me gripping adventures - some dangerous, some hilarious, but all filled with nostalgic memories.

Tillenius at work on the Wood Bison Diorama at the Canadian Museum of Nature in Ottawa. He was always very particular about the positioning of the mounted animals and would mould their stances in plasticine for the taxidermist and provide many detailed sketches of exactly the way the animal should be positioned. Note the plasticine cougar made by the artist and then note the positioning of the mounted animal as it is in the finished diorama.

In Cougar Country 20x54" oil collection of Mr. Lloyd J. Simmons

About to Turn 20x49" oil collection of Mr. and Mrs. George and Minnie Friesen

The Coming Challenge 20x54" oil collection of Mr. and Mrs. George and Minnie Friesen

During the time that Tillenius was researching and carrying out the studies for the Buffalo Hunt diorama at the Museum of Man and Nature he made thousands of drawings and paintings; some with only a slight change: the angle of the head of one animal or another, the color of the horse being ridden or the angle of the gun in the rider's hand and many more subtle changes that one can barely discern on these small canvases, which are usually four feet by six feet, but on the large scale that the diorama was constructed with a background painting fifty-two feet around these four by six canvases or panels were like smaller sketches for the original. Thirty years later the artist has been able to work some of these original drawings into finished paintings. Details from two of these: Metis Buffalo Hunt collection of the Museum of Man and Nature and Thunder of Hooves of a private collection., are shown here. The one he is working on, now resides in The Manitoba Club.

Master Design for the Red River Buffalo Hunt Diorama 24x72" oil collection of the Pavilion Gallery Museum Inc.

The Queen opening the Museum of Man and Nature with the diorama created by Tillenius in the background.

Tillenius on a walkway above the buffalo corrals in Elk Island National Park, Alberta 1993

Sometimes the buffalo refuse to go through the chutes and rear up, breaking through the top and appear uncomfortably close to those on the walkways above.

63

Tillenius creating the beginning stages of the background painting in his Winnipeg studio for the Inuit diorama. Then the canvas was rolled and transported to Baker Lake, N.W.T., where it was glued on the curved background.

Foreground rocks and moss placed in front of the painting so that Tillenius can match the colors and texture of the background.

Boris Kotelowich and Clarence Tillenius in front of the diorama in Baker Lake.

*Helen Steinkopf and Clarence Tillenius
collecting rocks and moss*

*Clarence and Boris out collecting rocks and moss for the foreground
of the diorama: Baker Lake townsite is in the background.*

Inuit carpenters helping with the base construction of the diorama

Baker Lake Lodge provided comfortable surroundings for Tillenius while working on the diorama, May-June 1998

Tillenius accepted, in 1997, an invitation to come to Ottawa to celebrate the 85th. birthday of the Victoria Memorial Museum Building which houses the Canadian Museum of Nature. While there he lectured on the dioramas and gave a drawing demonstration. On this occasion the President and Chief Executive Officer Ms. Joanne V. DiCosimo on behalf of the Canadian Museum of Nature presented Dr. Tillenius with an honorary membership and "a heartfelt thank you for (his) lifelong contribution to promoting an appreciation and respect for beauty of the natural world."

Everyone dressed in the costumes of the period when the building first opened, 85 years before as shown by John Kubicek and Marie-Claude Asselin.

Jacob Berkowitz, Clarence Tillenius, John Kubicek and Marie-Claude Asselin at the museum in Ottawa.

Tillenius in front of the Canadian Museum of Nature in Ottawa.

The trip to Ottawa was not all work, as can be seen from the expression as the artist delights in the ice cream treat. An enlargement of the sweet repast is really called for as it seems a work of art in itself.

*Pronghorn Antelope
diorama, Winnipeg*

Tillenius arranging Wood Bison Bull for diorama in Ottawa

*Dall Sheep
diorama Ottawa*

*Grizzly
diorama Ottawa*

*Polar Bear
diorama Manitoba*

Tillenius Dioramas

in chronological order over the peroid of 1962 to 1998

1. Fundy Bay Moose, Canadian Museum of Nature, Ottawa, Ontario
2. Dall Sheep, Canadian Museum of Nature, Ottawa, Ontario
3. Barrenground Caribou, Canadian Museum of Nature, Ottawa, Ontario
4. Grizzly Bear, Canadian Museum of Nature, Ottawa, Ontario
5. Pronghorn Antelope, Canadian Museum of Nature, Ottawa, Ontario
6. Cougar, Canadian Museum of Nature, Ottawa, Ontario
7. California Bighorn, Provincial Museum, Victoria, British Columbia
8. British Columbia Moose, Provincial Museum, Victoria, British Columbia
9. Coastal Forest Elk, Provincial Museum, Victoria, British Columbia
10. Buffalo Hunt, Museum of Man and Nature, Winnipeg, Manitoba
11. Pronghorn Antelope, Museum of Man and Nature, Winnipeg, Manitoba
12. Polar Bear, Canadian Museum of Nature, Ottawa, Ontario
13. Wood Bison N.W.T. Canadian Museum of Nature, Ottawa, Ontario
14. Rocky Mt. Goat, Provincial Museum, Edmonton, Alberta
15. Polar Bear, Museum of Man and Nature, Winnipeg, Manitoba
16. Barrenground Caribou, Museum of Man and Nature, Winnipeg, Manitoba
17. Boreal Forest Moose, Museum of Man and Nature, Winnipeg, Manitoba
18. Inuit Caribou Hunt, Cultural Heritage Centre, Baker Lake, Northwest Territories.

The Story Behind the Painting
told by the Artist

Tillenius paintings have a story that may be as interesting as the painting itself - Tillenius often writes letters to the owners if he thinks they would appreciate the story behind their painting such as the following one.

Mercy Flight   *oil private collection*

In 1950 I was living in East St. Paul on the Red River: one evening I had a phone call from Art Richardson of Richardson Brothers Art Gallery. He said: "A gentleman from Kentucky was in the gallery today who has seen your big moose and wolves painting in the Legislative Building: he is staying tonight at the Fort Garry Hotel and would like to talk to you about painting a wolf hunting canvas for him. Will you call him?"

That is how I met James Clay Ward of Kentucky who became a close friend over the years: his death some years after was a sad happening: he was a friend much missed. He had built a large camp on Tetu Island on the Winnipeg River where he was accustomed to fly in groups of his friends from Kentucky and having seen my moose and wolves painting, he now asked me to fly out to his lodge with him for a couple of weeks to get to know the country I would be painting.

His business was insuring high-profile racehorses for Lloyds of London: he had a beautiful home at Paris, Kentucky, only a short drive from Lexington where he took me to see the famous statue of Man O'War and to meet his friends, the executives of the exclusive Keeneland Racing Club, since beside painting wolves hunting he wanted me to become a painter of race horses as well.

I told him that I was a painter of wild animals, that painting wolves, moose and deer lay within my chosen field but racehorses and the race track would mean setting aside my true love, painting wild animals and wilderness.

Since painting race horses was not to be, Clay accepted this with good grace and said: "Well, O.K. we'll forget the racetrack for now. However, if I lay on a plane and pilot for you and a second plane and pilot for me, will you agree to come out to my Tetu Island camp at intervals for the next few years and paint whatever you like. But particularly I want that wolf, deer and airplane painting and whatever you paint just HAS to be authentic."

Well that's the story of how the canvas came to be painted.

Just realized, I haven't told you of the various misadventures this painting went through in the process of getting painted. When I first arrived at Clay's lodge on Tetu Island, I spent several days on snowshoes tracking wolves as far as where the English River flowage comes into the main river and at one place I found the tracks of a deer pursued by the wolf pack and later the kill.

Some time later, back in my Winnipeg Studio I worked up a canvas of a wolfpack closing in on a doe at the eastern end of Tetu Island, with a glimpse of Little Island beyond. I had this canvas (forgot the size, I think it was a 22x36) about half-finished when I got a phone call from Clay (who was sword-fishing in the Bahamas) saying he was leaving for his Winnipeg River Lodge the next day and could I take the train and meet him in Kenora where he wanted to pick-up his team of Siberian huskies and their trainer and we would fly out together in the same small plane.

Well, I had wanted to check with Tony Savoyard (who was leader of a native work group from the Ojibway reservation

In At The Kill 20x28" oil

at White Dog, farther (about 8 miles) up the Winnipeg River) to see if my placing on the wolves attacking the doe was in his opinion the way they usually went about it.

Well, when we got on the plane the 5 huskies immediately got into a ferocious dog fight. I was holding my wet canvas to protect it, but got it behind me, grabbed the collar of one dog with my one hand, kept another dog at bay by kicking at his face (no seats, small plane, I was sitting on the cabin floor). Beside the dog fight, the huskies were terrified of the bumpy plane ride - which loosened their bowels all over the plane - so when we landed at Clay's sumptuous lodge on Tetu Island I said to Clay "What more can an artist do to paint a picture?"

Tony Savoyard then looked at the partly-laid-in canvas and said "Deer good, wolves good, but you got one wolf up front - wolf don't do dat deer might strike with front hoof, if wolf g e t

cripple, can't hunt goin' to starve. No, wolf bite from side, or catch leg, that way he don't get hurt but pull deer down!"

So with Tony's expert criticism I re-positioned the lead wolf, finished the painting and sent it off to Clay who was delighted with it, and asked if I would undertake several more so that he could leave a painting to each of his married daughters and their children. Well, over the years I did finish some others (though I was on a very heavy work schedule on other projects much of the time) and was in fact at work on another episode Clay had witnessed of a cow moose defending her new-born calf from an attacking blackbear when word reached me of Clay's untimely death. I have those sketches yet but never completed the painting. I forgot to mention Clay had also bought the big painting of moose and wolves he had first seen in the Manitoba Legislative Building.

Wolves, Whitetails and Wood Buffalo 24x48" oil collection of the Pavilion Gallery Museum Inc.

His Mountain Kingdom 28x40" oil private collection

Herd Master Aroused 36x48" oil

These two views of the same painting show the detail of the bull elk and the overall design

Fox by Old Den Tree 27x36" oil

Challenge From Below - Rival Bull Approaching   48x72" oil

Young Grizzly Exploring 16x20" oil

Elk Herd and Packtrain 48x72" oil

Grizzlies in Red Rock Canyon 24x36" oil

Black and White in the Green Forest 10x20" oil

Inuit Polar Bear Hunt 25x36" oil collection of Jotrin Investments Ltd.

The Spirit Bear
by Clarence Tillenius
Inuit hunters of Southampton Island in the Canadian Arctic demonstrate for an artist the hunting of the white bear.

Our dog teams were trotting briskly along the frozen Kokumiak River when suddenly the husky leading the teams, a big white male, threw up his head with a growl and stopped, his muzzle pointing towards the snow cornice crowning the cliff towering above us. "Nanook!" ("The White Bear") muttered tracker Nakoolak, tough and weathered leader of the polar bear hunters I was travelling with.

In a moment the Inuit hunters anchored two dog teams with their sleds to the river ice and unloaded while we took off with the other two teams and empty sleds on a slanting path up the cliff face to where we could now see the dark opening of a polar bear den in the face of the 10-foot snowdrift overhanging the precipice.

As we shuffled in our slippery sealskin kamiks over the crusted snowdrift on the canyon rim we could see a few feet below us the entrance to the bear's den in front of which a dozen dogs were now snarling and barking. As though in answer, a new and ominous sound reached us, a steady growling like thunder under our feet. It was the bear, threatening with instant annihilation any dog bold enough to enter his sanctuary.

The Inuit indicated by signs the danger of walking over the snowdrift under which crouched the bear, because at the sound of footsteps over the roof of his cave the bear might strike upwards, smash the snow crust and drag us down into the den with him. As the Inuit said in their limited English: "You not like that: that not nice!"

Now the hunters unhooked the dogs from one sled, and dragged it upside down over the snow roof of the bear den.

Before we set out on this hunt, friend Eric Mitchell had explained to the Inuit hunters (having been a Hudson's Bay Co. fur trader for many years, he was

Impasse - Dog Team at Chasm Edge 36x48" oil collection of the Pavilion Gallery Museum Inc.

Mama's Defender 15x30" oil

Polar Bear Leaping at Diving Seal 15x30" oil

Showing the Cubs Their Kingdom 30x24" oil
collection of Brian Owen and Valerie Anne-Owen

Winter Seacoast - In the Violet Dusk 36x48" oil collection of Mr. and Mrs. George and Minnie Friesen

fluent in the Inuktitut language) that I was an artist, a painter of animals. Furthermore, that I had been commissioned to do two large museum dioramas of polar bears in the Arctic and wanted to see exactly how these experienced old bear hunters went about their hunt, so I could paint the scenes.

The Inuit hunters promised that if we found a bear in a situation where they could do it, they would tackle their quarry with a spear so I could see how it was done in the old days. In a brief consultation among themselves, they now decided this was such a situation.

Sateeana had stationed himself at one side of the cave entrance with his spear poised, then muttered a command to the dogs clamoring at the den. By far the most savage of the dogs was a lean black and white bitch and the next thing I knew she had disappeared inside the den and was snarling into the bear's face.

With a roar the bear burst out and Sateeana drove the harpoon into his neck. Like a striking rattlesnake the bear whipped around and bit the spearshaft in two, retreating back into his cave with the harpoon point sticking in his neck.

Sateeana's brother Paniyuk handed him the second spear (they had only two) and Sateeana took up his former stance beside the den mouth. The fierce black and white bitch, several of the other dogs pushing after her, made another rush into the bear's den taunting him. In a bound the bear

came out, saw Sateeana, and before the hunter could launch his spear the bear struck it from his grasp to send it sailing over the cliff and down the quarter-mile slope below. The bear once more backed into the den. Both spears gone, the bear enraged and growling in his den, what to do now?

The Inuit held a soft-voiced colloquy. Sateeana made a noose at one end of his 30-foot sealskin dog-whip and fastened that to the end of the bitten-off harpoon shaft. Eecherk harnessed

the loose dogs to the other end of the sealskin rope and Paniyuk, now lying spread-eagled on the top of the overturned sled on the den roof, scratched a hole in the snowcrust and looked down through it. Sateeana pushed in his noose along the bear den floor as far as the shaft allowed.

The hunters gestured to me by signs that when the snarling black and white bitch irritated the bear into lunging forward, Paniyuk with his eye at the peephole would see when the bear put his foot in the noose: he would signal and Sateeana would flip up the noose (catching the bear's foot), Eecherk would drive the dogs forward and the bear would be pulled into the open. The harnessed dogs were now writhing and twisting with eagerness, jumping about with half-smothered yelps and whines of anticipation.

The signal came, the dogs surged forward and Paniyuk with his eye at the den-roof peephole began to shake with uncontrollable laughter. What he had seen, and what the others did not know, was that the bear's foot was not caught at all: he was holding the noose with one claw and when the leaping dog team hit the end of the rope he straightened his

claw and the whole tangle of dogs barrelled head over heels over the cliff and down the slope. The Inuit thought this so absolutely hilarious they clutched their sides with laughter.

The crestfallen dogs after a bit came clawing their way back over the rim and Sateeana set about fashioning another noose. But as he approached the den and shoved the noose and shaft inside, the black and white bitch - beware the female of the species! - rushed past him into the den, the other dogs after her. With a bawling roar the bear charged irresistibly forward and in an instant bear and dogs were tumbling down the canyon wall to where the other two dog teams were tethered far below.

The next instant bear and dogs were fighting all over the sleds with their precious cargo. On the sleds were my spare camera, my caribou parka and sleeping robes and my sketching outfit. I mentally kissed the outfit goodbye as I saw the pandemonium of the dogs and bear slashing and tearing over the sleds.

We all started down the slope, the sealskin soles of our kamiks slipping and sliding uncontrollably on the steep and icy slope, and we had just reached a narrow ledge half way down when we realized the bear had beaten the dogs off and was now scrambling up the slope straight toward us.

We could not climb back up - our boots were too slippery - we could not go down because there came the bear: altogether the situation was one where as the French phrase it: "It gave us furiously to think."

Fortune favored us. As the bear approached closer, the steepness of the slope immediately below us seemingly caused him to turn north along a lesser gradient which led away from us. The horde of dogs leaping and yelping around him troubled him not all save for hissing growls and an occasional snarl as he connected with a haymaker lifting an unwary dog in a fifteen-foot arc down the hill to land with a yelp and a resounding thump.

As the bear disappeared along the canyon rim I hurried down to the sleds, where the contents were strewn everywhere. Great was my relief when I saw that apart from a couple of rips in my caribou parka and some claw dents on my painting easel and outfit no lasting damage to the vital equipment had been done.

I now followed Sateeana who had taken the only rifle and was again on the track of dogs and bear. Here and there we could see a crippled dog lying on the snow (where the bear's lethal swings had connected) and soon we saw the bear who had halted under an overhanging snow cornice at the top of the ridge. He was flanked by two barking sled dogs, and directly in front of him was the savage black and white bitch as fiercely indomitable as before.

As we toiled slowly up and drew near the bear, his glinting eyes were steadily on us as we came and we knew he recognized that we, not the dogs for which he cared little, were the true enemy.

Sateeana nudged me and said " I shoot: he getting mad." The bear stood there on the snow pedestal, regal, magnificent, true embodiment of the awful majesty of the untamed Arctic. Must he die? Not for me: I should have willed him to live, monarch of his Polar wastes, harming no one, living his wild and lonely life, asking only to be left alone.

But it was the Inuit's hunt. They had hunted his kind for a thousand years, his fur and his flesh were their livelihood: why should this hunt be an exception?

So the rifle rang, the bear flinched, then stiffened and rolled down the hill leaving a long red roadway. Even as he stiffened in death a dog rushed in only to receive a last crippling blow from the giant paw before it was stilled forever.

Climbing down to where the dead bear lay, Sateeana signalled to his companions now gathering by the anchored sleds. Two of them came with harnessed dogs and looping a sealskin line around the bear's forepaws the dogs dragged him to the sleds. Here we made temporary camp and Sateeana and Paniyuk set about skinning the bear.

As they cut up the carcass and took out the entrails, Eecherk picked up the liver, walked over to a deep crack in the ice and dropped the liver out of sight. "Why throw away the liver?" I asked Eric. "Many bear livers are highly poisonous,", Eric replied: "the concentration of vitamin A is so deadly both men and dogs have died from eating it. At best they can be made deathly ill."

Eecherk returned and spoke briefly to Eric, who turned to me. "Many hunters say their dogs can tell which livers are poisonous, and will not touch them", Eric said, "but Eecherk says best not to take a chance: we just put it where nobody can get at it."

The Inuit hunters had now stowed away the skin of the first bear killed and in a small plywood boat lashed on top of the second sledge they had packed the meat. "What is the boat for, on a bear hunt?" I asked Nakoolak. "Mebbe shoot seal: need boat," he replied, motioning me to climb aboard the sledge as the dogs set off. Two sledges had already gone to pick a site and build an igloo for the night. When we reached it, bone-weary from the strenuous day we rolled in our sleeping furs and knew no more till the sound of yelping dogs and cracking whips woke us to a new day.

Grey overcast and a cutting, bitter wind greeted us as we stepped out of the igloo. The Inuit hunters, working steadily, loaded the sleds and as a final touch lashed caribou skins on top to sit on. At a low-voiced command, the dogs from each team gathered around their owner and as they were harnessed each took his accustomed place in front of the sledge behind the leader.

As we slowly progressed up the long slope toward the height of land the overcast cleared and the sun came out, but if anything the day turned colder, the bitter, bitter wind in our faces. Now and then we struck patches of deep soft snow where the dogs, panting heavily and tongues hanging out, strained to their utmost to drag the sledges upwards.

In mid-morning the Inuit called a halt to rest the straining dogs and to re-ice the frozen mud coating of the sled runners. Paniyuk set up and lit the primus stove to melt snow for tea-water. Sateeana and Eecherk set about unloading the sleds and turning them upside down. Nakoolak took a piece of polar bear fur and, dipping it in a pan of the now boiling water ran it down the frozen mud surface of the sled runners, leaving a thin film of ice. "Make sled run more easy," said the Inuit to my query, as Paniyuk began ladling out tea and hot caribou broth.

Refreshed and eager, the dogs broke loose the sleds and in another half hour we had crossed the height of land with a wonderful panorama spread before us. The hunters paused here just long enough for me to make a hasty carbon pencil sketch for a possible diorama background, then one after another the dog teams started down the miles-long steep slopes ahead. Immediately troubles of another sort beset us. As the heavy sledges picked up speed on the steep downgrade even the madly galloping dogs could not keep ahead and now and then an unfortunate animal stumbled and was run over by the downrushing sled. The Inuit hunters threw themselves from side to side jerking the sleds by the rope lashings to avoid hitting rocks which knocked chunks out of the frozen mud runners. At the lip of a vast valley the lead team pulled up and we all stopped alongside. The Inuit hunters conferred briefly together, then Sateeana left them, coming over to Eric gesturing to the valley ahead.

"He says," Eric interrupted, "that they are going to unhook the dogs and ride the sleds down alone. The pitch is too steep: the dogs would be run over, crushed and killed. We Kabloonas

absolute masters of their sleds these Inuit were. By a deft twitch this way or that on the ropes attached to the front end of the runners, the rider could make the sled swing right or left at will. When it seemed to be accelerating at too dizzying a speed, the rider pulled hard on right or left rope and , as the sled responded, jerked hard on both ropes together. The heavy sled runners with nearly a thousand pound load, dug into the rock hard snow surface like a skier "stemming", the sled would plow to an abrupt stop sending up a shower of snow and ice particles and the next instant with ropes released the sled was shooting downward as before.

So fascinated was I watching this amazing sled trajectory down the chasm I had forgotten Eecherk's dogs. Huddled together and howling disconsolately as their masters disappeared down into the void, they began running around the steep chasm walls below. We had thought they would accompany us, but they had no faith (and less liking) for us Kabloonas. With despairing yelps one after another let go their precarious perches and fell, tumbled and rolled down onto the waiting rocks beneath. Bruised and yelping, they picked themselves up at the bottom and galloped to rejoin their Inuit masters now waiting by their sleds, looking as small as ants on the distant valley floor. Slipping, scrambling and heavily falling, we at length made our way down by the circuitous cliffside route and rejoined the party.

The beauty of the scene before us was beyond description. The reddish granite rocks, spotted here and there with yellow, black and grey lichens, glowed rust-red, scarlet and orange in the low afternoon sun. Under a pale green and golden sky the shadows on the snowy hillsides and distant ranges flowed in shades of pale blue, lilac and lavender: the snowbanks , where they caught the light, were creamy pink. Alternatively I trotted beside the dogs or sat on the sled drinking in the gorgeous vistas, each more beautiful than the last, promising myself that one day I would re-create them all on canvas.

(white men) are to make our way down as best we can making a long circle to the left and climbing down the rock terraces. Their dogs will make their way down somehow, the hunters will wait for us down on the valley floor."

With this we moved ahead a few rods and stopped in shock. Immediately in front of us was a yawning blue chasm, like the vortex of a volcano, the walls dropping almost sheer for perhaps an eighth of a mile. Even while we watched, Eecherk gave his sled a push and leaped astride it as it careened down the almost vertical wall. Now we had a chance to see what

A shout from Sateeana disturbed my reverie. "Nanook!" Ahead of us in a overhanging snow cornice was unmistakeably a bear den: Sateeana let loose his dogs. They rushed up the slope, Sateeana hurrying after: suddenly they jumped back. What looked like a bear's head all of a sudden appeared in the opening. Next minute a shout of laughter: the seeming "Bear" was Sateeana's yellow-white dog which had walked over the roof of the den - only a few inches thick here - and fallen through.

We were laughing over this incident when we heard shouting from the opposite ridge: "They see a bear!" It was Nakoolak and his dogs on the far crest and now we could see in the distance his dogs milling around a long snowdrift.

Gasping and sweating, lungs laboring, kamiks slipping, we struggled through hip deep snow in the ravine and up the far slope. On the mountain top stood Nakoolak and just beyond him his dogs, barking and leaping furiously in a ring around a deep trench in the snow. In the trench, which was like an extended snow-cave with no roof, was the bear, angrily hissing.

As we came nearer the dogs redoubled their attacks, and the bear, now growling furiously, lunged out of his trench singling out individual dogs for attack and backing into his cave, rump first, after each savage rush.

Though we expected Nakoolak to shoot the bear he made no move to do so: the other hunters were still some distance off, and gradually the dogs seemed to lose interest and wandered off, leaving at last only Nakoolak's black and white dog still circling the bear.

The bear now turned his eyes on us and the thought came to me that if the bear chose this moment suddenly to leap out of his trench and attack us we would have little chance, unarmed as we were. But the bear showed no sign of aggression except a low growling deep in his throat which we interpreted as: "Keep your distance or you will regret it."

While puzzling over Nakoolak's apparent indifference to the bear we saw Paniyuk climbing up carrying a rifle. At a word

from Nakoolak, Paniyuk walked towards the bear, raising the rifle. As he approached, the bear half reared as though to spring when the black and white dog suddenly attacked. The bear whipped around to strike at the dog just as Paniyuk fired, breaking the bear's back. At the sound of the shot, the dogs came rushing back at the bear. Crippled as he was, he fought furiously and the roaring and growling of the bear mingled with the frenzied yelping of the dogs was mounting to a crescendo when Paniyuk's rifle spoke again and all was over.

The Inuit hunters, who now had all arrived, took hold of the dead bear's paws and all together with a mighty heave swung him out of the trench and with another concerted heave started the heavy body sliding head first down towards the valley, Sliding and tumbling, the bear careened wildly down the slope to fetch up at last against a rock near where Eecherk's dog team and sled were tethered.

Now it seemed to be Eecherk's bear - though how the Inuit worked out who owned what bear on a hunt like this I was never able to fathom, for Nakoolak *found* the bear, Paniyuk *killed* it, and yet Eecherk now seemed the owner. Eecherk fastened the bear behind the sled, started the dogs, and all bore away down the valley to where it was decided we would camp.

All along the cliffs flanking the valley were a number of huge rock monoliths set up on boulders, sometimes on 3, sometimes on 4. They seemed to have been placed by human agency, but

so large were some of these rocks (and by the incrustation of lichens they must have been there untold centuries) - that we asked the Inuit what they were and who put them there. "The Tunit," (a legendary race of giants) answered the Inuit, and that was that.

I had made a side expedition to sketch some of these strange rock set-ups, and when I reached camp it was dark. Under the brilliant white light of a Coleman lantern hung on a harpoonshaft Sateeana was skinning the bear and Paniyuk, the acknowledged expert among experts in igloo building, was setting the snow blocks in place for an igloo he assured us would be the best we had yet seen on this trip.

So it proved, for it was over 14 feet long and had two sleeping benches, each facing the other across a central passage way, so that for the evening we could all sit facing each other for a most interesting story-telling night.

In spite of the strenuous day and the frightful cold of one of the bitterest nights we had had, marvellous light effects of the Inuit hunters working under the wonderfully dramatic light of that Coleman lantern excited me to the degree I could hardly leave off watching until both cheeks were again frozen which one of the hunters pointed out to me, at the same time gently nudging me towards the igloo. An odd incident now occurred. All previous nights the rifle had been left outside so that warm moist air inside would not condense and freeze and perhaps jam the action, but now Paniyuk, with a muttered comment unintelligible to me, picked up the weapon and followed me into the igloo with it.

Inside the igloo, what a contrast with the deadly cold outside! - the sleeping benches covered with deep-furred hides of caribou and polar bear: the tea kettle and the stew pot steaming over the kudlik (stone cooking lamp) and a tot of hot buttered rum saved for just such an occasion.

After the meal and a general loosening of belts we sat in an irregular circle and in the genial glow of the overproof rum and the hearty stew, the hunters' diffidence gave way to an expanding geniality, and hesitantly the stories began. Before the story-telling could properly begin a necessary ceremony was enacted: an empty gallon lard pail was passed around the circle, each contributor relieved himself, and the now-full lard pail was emptied against the igloo wall behind the snow

sleeping bench where it froze like stone on the instant.

Now the stories began: and what tales they were! Not only of personal exploits - though these were not lacking, and engrossing they were, with the intent dark faces leaning forward and the flickering lamp throwing fantastic shadows on the igloo walls.

First came the tale of Sateeana's dog falling through the roof of the bear den and reappearing in the den opening to the astonishment of Sateeana and his dogs: the salvoes of laughter which erupted at Sateeana's witty recital of this episode triggered a reminiscence by Eecherk. His experience, as near as I recall Eric's translation, was like this: his dogs scented a bear in his snow cave on top of a cliff. Before Eecherk reached the spot his lead dog incautiously walked over the roof of the snow cave. Hearing the footsteps the bear smashed through

the hard snow crust and with his formidable claws hooked the dog down into the den and slashed his side open. The dog sprang for the opening and had almost made it up out of the cave when the bear dragged him down again and worked him over. A second time the dog almost made it up out of the den when the bear seized him yet again. This time no dog reappeared: instead the bear suddenly stood up on his hind legs, head and shoulders above the cave roof. Eecherk who had just arrived swung up his carbine and fired: the bear fell down into the den.

Eecherk approached the hole and looked down: the bear lay on his side on top of the dog: neither was moving. Reaching down and poking the bear with his rifle brought no reaction, so Eecherk jumped down into the cave and with a supreme effort hauled the bear's heavy body off the motionless dog. The dog's scalp was torn loose and hung over his eyes: there were deep slashes along his sides where the ribs showed, but when Eecherk laid his ear against the dog's side he could hear the heart faintly beating.

This was one of his best dogs, his lead dog, and Eecherk would not willingly lose him. He hauled the dog free, lifted him out, and from his sled got a needle and sinew. In a few minutes he had sewed the scalp back in place, stitched up the other wounds and set out for the settlement. Inuit dogs are unbelievably tough: they have to be, only to stay alive in that harsh environment. Certainly this dog was: he not only recovered but lived a long time thereafter as Eecherk's top dog.

At a lull in the story-telling, I asked "When you talk of big bears, just _how_ big is a _big_ polar bear? With one accord, all the hunters turned towards Eecherk, the youngest hunter of the group, and said: "Eecherk killed the biggest bear."

Eecherk took up the story: "I was hunting with my brother on the ridges along the sea-coast: we came upon a bear. He stood above us on a high ridge: I could see he was big: _how_ big, I was later to find out. The dogs were all barking at the foot of

the cliff when I fired, and fired again. The bear fell straight down among the dogs and as they closed in, he seized one and bit him completely in half. He got up and started running. I fired again and again, hitting him each time until he fell. The dogs closed in again and though he was dying he struck one last blow. It tore away the dog's whole shoulder blade and part of his rib cage. He was the biggest bear I have ever seen, but he cost me two of my best dogs." The other Inuit nodded assent: "Ee, (yes) it was the biggest bear any of us have ever seen: we have never seen a greater."

As story followed story, the themes gradually shifted to tales of the supernatural, to these Inuit hunters not supernatural at all, but simply events controlled and brought about by "magic". Such as the bear spirit wrestling with a lost man, turning him into a bear, the man struggling and regaining his human form only to be overcome again by the bear spirit and finally being tracked and found by his searching companions naked, dead and frozen in the snow far from his village which in his agony he had tried to reach.

The stories went on - fascinating - but the day had been long and strenuous: the story-telling grew desultory and one by one we sought our sleeping bags.

One question, though, intrigued me: in all the weeks on the trail, this was the first night the Inuit had brought the rifle into the igloo: what was their reason?

The Inuit at first seemed reluctant to answer but finally Sateeana made a lengthy speech to Eric, who translated: "This valley we are camped in tonight is not an ordinary valley: down this valley come many, many bears on their way to the sea. Sometimes it happens that among these many bears there comes one who is not an ordinary bear but a spirit bear. He is huge, he is resistless: at sight of him the dogs, who bark without stopping when any ordinary bears come, now fall silent and cower away: they know he is something more than mortal, and they fear. And such a bear cares nothing for the dogs, he walks through them and past them as though they do not exist: he cares nothing for men either, and should such a bear come, he would smash this igloo (and us) if it is in his way and continue on his way to the sea."

"But do you think such a bear might come?" I queried. "We do not know", was the answer, "but the bear we killed this afternoon was a strange bear. He did not attack any of you when you stood by his trench after the dogs had gone: he had not made a cave but a kind of open ditch: he did not attack Paniyuk when Paniyuk raised his rifle but turned on the dog instead: even when his back was broken he fought as fiercely as before: we do not know: there is something strange here."

I asked no more, but in my mind I saw again the bear as we had come upon him that afternoon on the mountain top with that wonderful light effect over the landscape behind him: so regal, so magnificently a part of his arctic kingdom - and now his hide lay packed in Eecherk's boat on top of man-high snow pillars out of reach of the dogs he had despised in life.

Half dozing, half dreaming that I was again on the open hillside with the bear turning his gaze from the dogs to me, I finally fell asleep. In the morning I awoke to a day of searing cold, brilliant sunshine, my companions up and stirring. No spirit bear had come to avenge his fallen comrade: the igloo was unbroken, and today we would resume our journey to the sea, where we now discovered the fresh trail of a huge bear leading on before us.

Of the many canvases I have painted of the Arctic and its dwellers, the scenes and experiences of this expedition live in memory: in Canada's National Museum and Manitoba's Museum of Man and Nature are the polar bear dioramas I created from the scenes witnessed on this trip and others like it.

Of all the episodes I witnessed, the scene pictured in my canvas "Inuit Polar Bear Hunt" is the one etched forever in my memory: Sateeana poised with his harpoon, the black and white bitch taunting her adversary, and the furious charge of the great white bear himself, the apotheosis of life and death.

CUBBY.

C.J. Fillenius. 34.

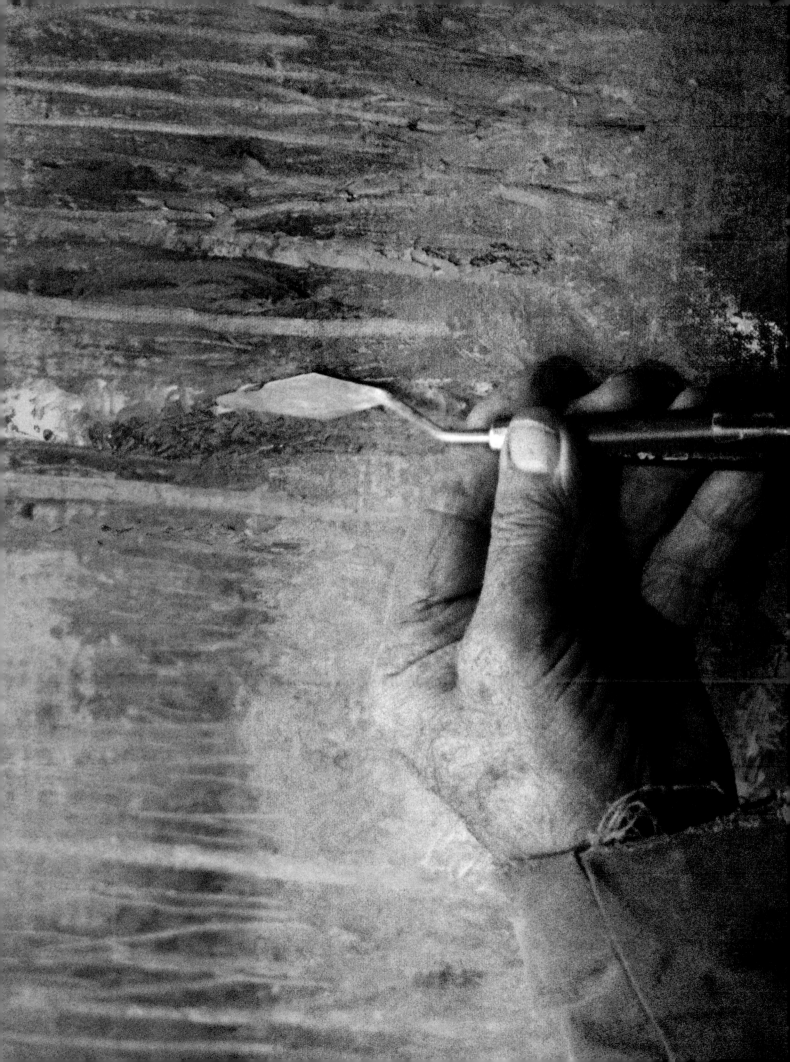